TO

TELLS IT STRAIGHT

With Love

TOMA
TELLS IT STRAIGHT
With Love

BY DAVID TOMA
with IRV LEVEY

JAN
PUBLISHING

I want to give special thanks to my wife Pat and my kids, Jimmy, Patty Ann, Donna, and Janice for all the love and patience that has enabled me to continue my work. But I can never thank enough all of the millions of kids throughout America who so greatly motivated me to write this book.

I love you all.

Manufactured in the United States of America

Library of Congress Catalog Card Number 81-68081

ISBN: 0-916728-55-2

JAN Publishing
21 West 26 Street
New York, New York 10010

Design by Robert J. Luzzi

ACKNOWLEDGMENTS

Front cover photo: Bill Powers, Police Magazine
Page 48:   Family Album
Pages 18, 20, 26, 28, 32:   Universal Studios
Page 140:   Ace Alagna
Page 36, 164:   Bill Powers, Police Magazine
Pages 75, 82, 86, 88, 94, 140, 104, 114, 128, 190:   Allison Show

TOMA
TELLS IT STRAIGHT
With Love

CONTENTS

INTRODUCTION

This book could save your son or daughter's life and it can save your family! David Toma—an American hero—knows more about street drugs than anyone else in the country. He has been fighting drugs and working with kids in the schools for over 20 years. We had all better listen when he tells us that over 80% of our school kids are fast slipping to self-destruction with drugs, alcohol and suicide. They are losing their memories, their powers of concentration, and their ability to function. The drugs, mostly marijuana, are blocking their emotional and mental growth.

No one knows it as well as David Toma—and no one *reaches* kids the way Toma does. He speaks to over one million kids and adults a year, in schools throughout the country. Many thousands of young people have turned off drugs after spending a single day with him. He has hundreds of thousands of letters from kids and parents that documents his effectiveness. He teaches almost immediately how to get high on life, which in his words is, "the only way to get high."

Toma, a living legend, is a former police detective and probably the most famous cop in the world. Two television series, "Toma" and "Baretta," and three books have been based on his heroic exploits as an undercover cop in Newark, New Jersey. He took on the world in a one man war for his own survival, and he did survive! He was shot, stabbed, and hospitalized over 30 times in the line of duty, yet he never fired his gun at anyone. He's a self-made man, who strives to excel in all he does, and his talents are many. He's been a boxer, a marine drill instructor, a baseball player, and a musician.

Many parents will be shocked to learn of the drug epidemic—many will refuse to believe it could be happening throughout America's school system and, yes, to their own children. But those who truly love their children will want to learn all they can about the crisis and how to fight it. Toma will show you how millions of kids are being held hostage by drugs and alcohol, and how little, if anything, is being done to curb the epidemic.

In his book, you'll learn how a personal tragedy led Toma to his own addiction and how he was cured. You'll be with him in high schools as he shouts, ''Stop killing yourselves with that garbage! You're poisoning each other!'' You'll watch and learn why kids mob the stage after his four hour talk to get near him—to touch him. You'll hear them open their hearts in personal meetings with Toma. It will shock you and anger you but your eyes will be opened to what's happening in the schools. You'll discover what you can do for your kids, yourself, and your community, as you begin to understand Toma's special gift—the ability to reach a nearly lost generation, with a message of concern and love, hope and courage.

Yes, based on the statistics, your kids are probably experimenting with drugs now—with absolutely no idea of how dangerous they are.

In this book, you'll learn

- Why marijuana is a tremendously dangerous, unpredictable, and misunderstood drug that is wrecking kids *and* adults for life.
- How to stop your own drug and alcohol abuse, if you're now a user.
- How over 80% of high school kids—in big cities and small towns—get pressured into using drugs.
- Why marijuana and other drugs lead to mental disorder and to suicide.
- How to know for sure whether your kids are using drugs.
- and most important, how to help them stop their drug use, or prevent them from starting in the first place.

David Toma is the most dynamic and sought after speaker in America—at grammar schools, high schools and colleges; at corporations of all sizes and to organizations of all kinds. He speaks to standing room-only crowds and always receives thunderous standing ovations. His message is powerful and lasting. Toma touches the hearts of everyone he meets. Kids and parents love him. He uses all his talents—his flamboyancy, charisma, acting ability and anything else he might have to draw on to get his message across for the sake of all Americans.

PART I

HOW I AM DRAWN TO THE KIDS

This country is in trouble. There's an epidemic raging across this land and we can't pretend it isn't happening: we can't dig a hole and hide from it either.

There is hardly a family that will escape its poison if we don't wake up to the danger, and begin to fight it.

While the adults in this country have been obsessed with improving their lot in life, climbing the financial and social ladder, enhancing their lifestyle—the kids have been sucked into the most insidious drug culture that has ever existed on the face of this earth. And let me tell you something, it's costing us dearly. Drugs—mostly marijuana—are warping their values, crippling their bodies, killing their minds. They will be incapable of managing their own lives.

How in the hell will they be able to raise a family, manage a business, govern a nation?

We worry about the kids eating junk food and watching too much television—but we look the other way when they poison their bodies and their brains with chemicals that do not belong inside any human being.

There's an epidemic raging across this land and we can't pretend it isn't happening

We worry about the threat of communism and fascism and anarchy. Well, let me tell you something, my friends, our enemies don't have to figure out ways to destroy this country. All they have to do is wait. We're doing it to ourselves.

The six o'clock news isn't covering <u>this</u> story, and don't expect to find it on the front page of your daily newspaper. You know why? Because most of the media has swallowed its own line. They believe their own screwed up perception of what this country is all about. They are as hypnotized by the crap they shove down our throats as we are. Oh, they know we have problems all right—the economy, energy, the environment. But the scariest problem of all gets shoved into the back pages of the papers or maybe on an all night radio talk show when most of us are tossing and turning in our beds.

Plenty of adults are going to say that I'm exaggerating, overstating, crying wolf, all black and white. Well, here's an invitation to everyone who reads this book. Spend one day with me, in any school where I'm speaking—elementary, junior or high—city or suburban—public or private. Spend one day with me and listen. Listen to what the kids tell me about drugs and alcohol. The critics become believers fast. They may not accept what I say, but they'll believe the children.

How many of the skeptics will accept my invitation? A handful, maybe. Most of the rest won't have the time, or don't want to know, or just don't give a damn. The kids will know what I'm talking about. They will recognize the truths in this book and that's what matters most to me. They are the ones I love and want to help.

> This book will cause problems for those it helps. But the problems will be temporary. It will scare them. Disrupt their lives. They are going to need the love, support, understanding and protection of every person close to them—parents, friends, relatives, teachers, clergy.

If you are going to let me into your life, you should know who I am, where I'm coming from and what my credentials are. So let's get to it.

I don't fool myself. I know that no publisher would let me in the door—and thousands of kids wouldn't come to hear me talk—if my work as an undercover vice, gambling and narcotics detective hadn't received national attention, or if the two television series based on my life, TOMA and BARETTA, hadn't turned me into something of a celebrity. So I'll start off by telling you how I became a cop and how that career, a tragedy in my life and a teenage junkie, led me to the kids.

I'm the youngest of twelve children and grew up in the roughest section of one of the toughest cities in America, Newark, New Jersey. Drugs even then were as plentiful as candy and soda pop. Muggings, robberies, rapes and murders were everyday occurrences. And the victims weren't just names in a newspaper to my family. Too often they were people we knew. Neighbors, friends, relatives. The perpetrators of the crimes weren't strangers either. We rubbed shoulders with plenty of them. Cheap punks who slithered around the street looking for an easy mark, and bigtime gangsters who made headlines.

Winos slept on our sidewalks and junkies shot up in our doorway. Whores worked every corner and bar while their pimps cruised our neighborhood looking for recruits.

That's the neighborhood where my brothers and sisters and I grew up.

As far back as I can remember I wanted to be a cop. When I was little I used to fantasize about rescuing my Mom from a mugger or saving my sister from being raped. I imagined pulling down the peak of my hat, flashing my badge and drawing my trusty old 38. David Toma to the rescue! The daydreams ended by the time I was a teenager, but not the idea that I could protect the people I loved if I were a cop.

When I was twenty-one I joined the police force. Newark's finest.

I started off my career as a uniformed patrolman. I was on alternating shifts—8 to 4, 4 to 12, 12 to 8. It wasn't anything like I expected. Before my shoes were broken in, I knew that I didn't like the job. I'm not knocking the position, but for me it was too confining, too organized, too routine. I felt more like a foot soldier in bootcamp than a policeman.

Day after day I'd go home and complain to my bride—but it didn't occur to me to quit the job. By the time I completed my first year of service, Patty and I became parents. David Jr. was born.

I stayed on patrol for five years—five long years—never happy, always complaining. Then, finally, I decided to make a move, and took the exam to become a detective. When I passed I jumped with joy.

To tell you the truth, I wasn't so sure that I'd make it. And I was really excited when I was assigned to the Vice, Narcotics and Gambling Division.

For the first six or seven months I did a terrific job. They wanted the junkies and the whores off the street and I was hauling them in by the wagon load. But something began nagging at me. I felt uneasy. Once more, I wasn't happy.

I began to worry about myself. Maybe I made a terrible mistake when I joined the police force. Or worse than that, maybe I could not be happy in any job. I always thought of myself as an "up" person, so why in the hell was I always down?

One night, like many nights, I couldn't sleep. But instead of tossing and turning I got out of bed and went into the kitchen determined to think it through. I relived everything I did that day on the job, and the day before, and the day before that. What in the hell was I doing that was making me so unhappy? Suddenly the pieces started to fall into place—and by morning I knew what was driving me nuts.

It was the junkies. I mean, the effect our crackdown had on them.

At the time I didn't give a damn about them. To me, they were an insult to decent society. My concern was the community and my personal need to do something worthwhile. What I'm getting at is this: These kids didn't have the money to hire a lawyer, put up bail, pay a fine. Every cent they could scrounge went to feed their habit. So where did they get the dough to keep them on the streets where the junk is?

From their suppliers. They borrowed the money from them. And after the addict paid his dues to the legal system, do you think the Big Business Man who floated the loan said to his customer, "Hey, you're a nice junkie, I'll just write this off as a business expense?" No way, baby. The rule is you play and you pay. So where in the hell do you think these kids get the money to pay back the lenders?

I'll tell you where they get it—they get it from you and me. They mug us. They stick a knife in our ribs and take it. They break into our homes and steal it. Sometimes they blow our heads off. If they are young enough and still have their looks, they may be able to peddle their bodies for part of it. Boys and girls.

And what about those who can't raise the money for bail and can't get a lawyer or pay a fine? Well, they get tossed into jail—they pay their debt to society and come out good, decent citizens.

Like hell they do. They get educated in the can, but not the way we want them to. They learn new ways to get high, make more connections to get drugs, find out better ways to rip us off.

These thoughts nearly blew my mind. I wasn't helping society, I wasn't protecting my family. I wasn't doing a damned thing for anybody!

The next day I went to one of my bosses to tell him what was on my mind. I said, "We're playing a game, man. What the hell good are we doing? The junkies are multiplying like rats. I'm locking up the same kids, time and time again. You're trying to program me. You want me to be your puppet. I think it's wrong. I can't do it."

I was nearly in tears. I wanted so much to reach him. Then he did his number on me. "When are you going to learn to mind your own business? Your job is to obey orders. You're a radical, Toma. We need soldiers on this police force, not bleeding hearts. You wanna be a social worker? Go to college. You wanna stay on the force? Be a good soldier."

Good soldier? Bullcrap! What he meant was, "Be like me, don't give a damn." Be a good robot, that's what he meant.

Every day after that it was a struggle to go to work. Even worse than before. The image of Toma the Robot kept flashing in my mind, and it made me feel like a creep. When I came home after my shift I'd tremble with fury. Nobody gives a damn, nobody gives a damn!

It got to the point where Patty, my wife, couldn't stand my anger and my depression. "Either become one of them or quit the force," she told me. "You can't change the system and you can't go on like this." I knew that I couldn't become one of them and still be me. But as much as I hated it, I couldn't quit the force either.

Maybe I was expecting too much from the department. And let's face it, I was screaming that what we were doing was wrong, but I wasn't offering any alternatives. So I made up my mind that if I was going to have any impact on the department or anyone else, I'd better learn everything there was to know about the criminal world, especially the drug business and its customers.

"We need to love one another—we need to learn how to express our love."

I didn't know where to start, but I was sure of one thing. I wasn't going to learn what I needed to know as long as I was on the outside trying to look in. The Law Officer studying The Criminal wasn't going to do it.

While I was trying to figure out what to do, I was expressing my thoughts to everyone on the squad. They thought I was nuts. Sometimes our conversations turned into heated arguments, but most of the time they just shrugged and walked away, leaving me seething. It got to the point where most of the sixty-five detectives in my squad stopped talking to me altogether. I'd walk into the room and they'd clam up as if I wasn't there.

One day when I was really down I went to talk to my mother. My mother was an uneducated woman. She didn't know a psychologist from a podiatrist, but she could have taught the shrinks I know a few things. She knew how to listen. I told her some of what was going on, expressed my self doubts. She put her arms around me and said, "David, you have to do what you know is right. If you <u>know</u> it's right, how can it be wrong?"

A few days later my boss called me in.

"Toma, make it easy on all of us. Resign from the department."

"Resign? Why? I'm doing my job. I'm making all the arrests you ask for."

"Nobody wants to work with you," he said. "They think you're a radical, a troublemaker. You think you can manipulate us into running this department your way. Well, you're wrong. Thank God you're not in charge. You're too damned soft."

Too soft? What the hell was I asking? Maybe we could use a little discretion before we busted the kids—before their records grew to the length of your arm. Maybe figure out how to stop them before they turned into killers or zombies. Is that being too soft?. Is that so crazy?

I thought, "Screw you, mister, and screw the sixty-five robots you got working for you. I'm not quitting and I'm not changing, and one of these days you'll be bragging that David Toma worked for you." Well, I didn't quit, and I didn't change, but neither did he. And you can bet on it that he never bragged about working with David Toma.

All the years I worked the streets of Newark, I looked down at the street junkies like they were filth. I wondered what kind of crappy families they came from. I hated them. They dirtied my town.

It's a funny thing. Four of my nephews were dope addicts, but somehow I didn't connect them to the street kids. I was angry at them for the pain that they were causing my sisters and their families. As far as I was concerned they were lazy, rotten, selfish punks. There was no excuse for them. They came from good families, religious and hard working, and they disgraced us all.

When Ronnie, one of my nephews, an addict of many years at that time, came to me and said, "Uncle David, I'm in a jam. You're a cop, you got influence, help me. Please help me." I blew my top. "You bum, what are you trying to do, kill your mother? Straighten out, get a job. Prove to me that you're a man. Until you do, don't come crying to me for help."

Isn't that the way most of us treat people who get in trouble and come begging for help? We tell them, "Come back when you're not in trouble, when you don't need me—that's when I'll help."

My reaction to my nephew came back to haunt me, more than once.

Like I said, I always considered addicts the scum of the earth. When I'd catch one shooting up in some dingy hallway I'd want to shove the syringe down his throat. But once I made up my mind that I was going to learn everything I could about these people, I began to see them in a different way. I started to look into their faces. Sometimes I would get a glimpse of fear, and not just fear of me. Sometimes I saw loneliness and I'd get the feeling these kids wanted to be helped. But when I approached them, whatever I thought I read in their faces turned to suspicion. They weren't going to let me in. But it didn't matter. The feeling that I wanted to reach out to them began to build. And the feeling kept growing.

Reaching out was nothing foreign to me. I grew up in a house where it was a way of life, a responsibility.

My father was an Italian immigrant who never mastered the English language, but he managed to hold down two jobs every day of his life in order to keep my Mom and their twelve kids housed and clothed and well fed. He did what he had to do. He brought us into this world and he accepted his responsibility.

My father was an honest man who never put a dollar in his pocket that he couldn't declare in his income tax return. And he wouldn't tolerate any of his kids cheating or lying. Let me tell you, we knew better than to try it. Some of the men who came to this country on the same cattle boat as my father became rich and powerful and dirtied their souls doing it. Pop liked to tell me, "You can't sleep well when you got crooked money hidden under your mattress." And he slept like a baby. He rarely preached his values, he demonstrated them. He was a man.

It was my mother, though, who taught us about loving and caring. She hugged us and kissed us and told us that we were beautiful. And all of her children grew up like her in that respect. None of us are reluctant to express our emotions. We holler when we're angry, we cry when we're sad, and most of all, we're not afraid to express our love.

My mother was a remarkable woman. She was a Pentecostal missionary, and can you believe this: although she had a husband and a dozen kids, she devoted a couple of days a week to helping people outside the family. One week she'd do volunteer work in a mental institution or an old age home, the next week in an orphanage or a prison. Lots of times, she'd take me with her.

Her friends couldn't understand how she could give up so much precious time to strangers. In Italian, she'd explain. "Lonely, frightened people need someone to talk to, someone to listen to them." My mother was right, of course, but how many people are willing to listen? Where are the people who care? The truth is that too many people don't give a damn.

Let me tell you something about caring. It's a beautiful emotion, but it's not worth a damn to anyone but ourselves unless we are willing to translate it into helping.

A cop may cry when he busts a fourteen year old whore and finds out she's rotting with syphilis. His heart may break for her. It's a noble emotion, but if he doesn't do something to save that child, caring doesn't mean a thing.

Well, helping these kids wasn't an easy thing for me to do. They were hard to care about and they wouldn't take me into their confidence. When I approached them, they'd split or clam up. I was a cop, one they all recognized. They had no reason to trust me.

I decided that the only way I could do any good was to go after the big dealers. The mob. Try to dry up the supply of drugs that was being peddled on the street. But how in the hell was I supposed to do that? If I were a stranger I could move around in their world. Get into places no cop could go. Learn things no cop could learn. But the mob knew me better than the kids did. I grew up with a lot of them. I knew their families, they knew mine. Then I got a crazy idea.

When I decided to make my move I was too embarrassed to share the idea with Patty. Maybe she'd think I was nuts. Besides it was going to cost me some money. By now we had three kids and money wasn't that plentiful. Anyway, I went to a costume shop in New York City and bought an assortment of wigs, moustaches, beards and makeup. You didn't see it on TV, but that's how the Baretta character started. I rushed home, locked myself in the bathroom and stood in front of the mirror for hours practicing how to put a wig on and take it off; how to put a beard on and take it off. Every day for weeks I spent four or five hours experimenting with the makeup. Practicing. I learned how to make myself look younger or older, heavier. I practiced changing my voice, my posture, my walk. I stuck cotton in my cheeks and under my lips to change the contour of my face. And I got good at it. Really good. I mastered between twenty-five and thirty disguises, and each one now takes me about forty seconds to do. Maybe you have seen me demonstrate this on the Mike Douglas Show. But you've got to believe me, show business wasn't on my mind then.

My life was on the line, in more ways than one. Most of the time I couldn't carry a badge and a gun. You can't get near a big shot in the mob carrying a piece. If you're caught, you're a dead cop. So I learned how to survive without that kind of weapon.

Many times I protected myself with my hands. I became a tough street fighter, but most of the time I protected myself with my wits. I became sensitive to every sound, sight and smell around me. I learned how to disappear in a crowd. I bluffed my way out of a lot of tight situations when I could. When I couldn't, I begged, cried and prayed. There were times when I took a beating from some punk that I could have taken with one hand, but I couldn't afford to win.

Every day when I went out on the job, I'd drive around the area I was working. Get the feel of things. When I decided who I wanted to be, I'd pull into a driveway or an alley and in less than a minute I'd be that person. Maybe a preacher, sometimes a hippie, once in a while a female. You know what I look like, and you're probably thinking that no guy would go near a dame with a face like mine. Well, let me tell you, where I came from they went after anything.

Did this whole crazy scheme work? You can give odds on it. I was locking up the big pushers, the distributors, and some of the really big mob guys. I ran up the best arrest record in the history of the department. And more important than that, the conviction rate on my busts was 95%. When you know that the average conviction rate for a cop is about 15%, it sounds pretty damned impressive. Did this make me a hero in the department? Hell, no.

My boss would tell me, "You're making an ass out of yourself, Toma. You're making the whole department look foolish. You like dressing up like a woman? Join a queer show."

He wanted me out of the department in the worst way, but how do you get rid of a guy who's setting an arrest record that may never be matched?

Eventually, something began to sink into my thick skull that really hurt. No one could ever dry up the supply of narcotics that was coming into our city.

It didn't matter how hard I worked, how many beatings I took, how many arrests I made, I couldn't stop the traffic. No sooner did I put one big dealer out of business, two more moved in. As long as the customers were looking to buy, the suppliers would find a way to deliver the merchandise. And the customers were multiplying like rabbits. They were getting younger, too.

The customers are the ones who really bewildered me. I could understand the sellers. They were motivated by greed. But the buyers? How in the hell could so many of them waste their lives like this? All of their ambition, all of their energy, and all of their drive were directed toward one goal: to get enough drugs to get them through the day.

I began to spend more time in the streets with them. I really wanted to understand. This may sound phony, but I wanted to help them.

I had worked in the street for years but I never really got to know the addicts. Now that I was disguised as one of them, they began to open up to me. It nearly blew my mind when I found out I was wrong about them. I honestly thought they were ghetto kids who never had a

> **I spent every minute possible with these kids. I slept with them in doorways, in stinking filthy rooms in abandoned buildings, in the gutter.**

chance from the start. Kids who couldn't get through school if you gave them the answers to all the tests. I figured their parents, if they were still around, could probably be found hanging out on some other street—stoned or drunk. I was wrong. Plenty of them came from fancy suburbs and pretty little towns and farms. These kids didn't play in the sweltering streets in the summer. Many of their parents belonged to beach clubs and had been PTA members. They weren't deprived or battered. Lots of them took music lessons and went on vacations and started out as happy children. Why were they blowing their minds on drugs?

I spent every minute possible with these kids. I slept with them in doorways, in stinking filthy rooms in abandoned buildings, in the gutter. I didn't pop a pill or smoke a joint or shoot up but they didn't know it. I would psych myself up, work myself into a state, and make it appear that I was as stoned as they were. The more I learned about them, the more puzzled I was. I couldn't for the life of me understand why they did this to themselves, why they would choose to throw themselves away. Like they were garbage. I thought they had a choice.

Then, my friends, something happened to me. Maybe God wanted me to understand Maybe He thought, "Baby, you wanna know how it can happen? I'll show you."

One Sunday afternoon after an uneventful day on the street, I took a radio call, an emergency. I spun my car around and headed for an address not too many blocks from my home. A little black boy, three years old, was strangling on a piece of charcoal. When I got to the house, I thought the little boy was dead. His eyes were bulging and he wasn't breathing. I couldn't find a pulse. Somehow I dislodged the chunk of charcoal from his throat, and his mother let out a cry of relief. But I didn't feel relieved. I was sure that the boy was dead. I don't know why, maybe because I couldn't deal with the mother at that moment, but I pressed my mouth against his and started blowing air down his throat. I don't know how many times I did it, but I remember that between each breath I took I begged, "Come on, baby, come on." Suddenly, without a sign that it was coming, the little boy gasped. He was alive, by God, he was alive! I kept pumping air into him and a few minutes later he began to gag. I swept him up into my arms and ran for the car, his mother following. In minutes we were at the Newark City Hospital. Third floor, pediatrics. I stayed with the woman in the hall while doctors worked on her kid. An hour passed and finally the door opened and we got the word. The little boy was okay, he would live.

The mother and I hugged and kissed and both of us cried. Then I raced to the car again, this time in ecstasy. A kid was dying and I saved his life. I had never saved a baby before. I could hardly wait to get home to share my joy with Patty and our children. The moment I bolted through the door my wife knew this was a special day. I was radiating happiness, she said.

Pat and the kids had already started eating dinner, so I took my seat at the table and began giving a second by second account of the incredible event. As I was really getting into the story, my five year old, David Jr, started to gag. A piece of food was stuck in his throat. I told him to raise his arms and gave him a sharp smack between his shoulder blades. What the hell did I know? It had worked a thousand times before. He started gurgling and I panicked. I grabbed him by the shoulders and shook him. One of the other kids screamed at me, "Daddy, Daddy, what are you doing to David, you're going to kill him!" Patty became hysterical. I was hollering at David to cough. I didn't know what the hell I was yelling. One of our neighbors heard the racket and came running in. I had turned David upside down and was begging him to give up the food. The woman phoned emergency, something I should have done right away, and moments later they were at my door. Then we were at the hospital. The same hospital that I had taken the other little boy. Newark City Hospital, third floor, pediatrics. The same doctors were waiting for us. The medic had called ahead. They rushed my child into the operating room. This time I couldn't wait in the hall. This time I was crazy with fear. They opened David's throat, but the tracheotomy didn't help.

Less than one hour after I had saved the life of a three year old stranger, I watched my own little boy strangle to death.

Just some of the many disguises Toma used in his career as a police detective in Newark. The "Toma" and "Baretta" television series are based on Toma's real-life exploits.

David Toma, super-cop, the bravest detective in one of the toughest cities in the world, panicked when his son needed him most.

Why do I share this story with you? Why do I tell it in every school I appear? Two television series and three books tell the world how strong I am, how brave I am, how ingenious I am, how good I am. Until an hour before my son's death I was a powerful man. I could take a life if I had to. I had that right. And I could save one. I was a crime fighter and had the scars to prove how hard I fought. Hospitalized thirty-two times. My body is tattooed with scars from bullet and knife wounds, and I still get headaches from the four concussions I suffered at the hands of our enemies. But I was a survivor. I knew how to cope. Up to an hour before David Jr. strangled to death, that is.

I tell this story because I want the kids to know that there are no gods on the face of the earth. No perfect heroes. You know where we're perfect heroes? On TV, thirty minutes a week.

There's another reason I tell this story. So you'll understand how a man who hated narcotics with a passion and spent almost his entire life fighting it at all levels — how such a man could become a drug addict himself.

Toma as a priest

When the doctor who was working on David turned to me and I knew my son was dead, I exploded with rage. What kind of God would contrive such a sick plot!

He gave me the power to save a child's life. He gave me a few minutes to feel that power, to bask in it. Then he snatched my own kid away from me, as if to show me how frail and impotent I really was. If He had to prove something, why take it out on my kid? At that moment I hated God. Oh, how I hated Him.

> Our home became a mess. The children couldn't understand why their brother didn't come home. They wouldn't stop talking about him. A neighbor who stopped in to pay her respects wondered out loud what might have happened if I had called emergency right away instead of trying to help David myself. My wife began to fall apart. She probably would have had a total breakdown if I had been stronger. I mean, one of us had to keep things going, take care of the children. It wasn't me. I simply couldn't deal with what happened, so I buried myself in anger and hate — in pain, depression and self-pity. Isn't that what most of us do when we're in a situation that we can't handle, a reality we don't want to face? We get ourselves into a state where we can't think straight.

Pat couldn't stand my rage. She called a doctor and made an appointment for me but I didn't want to go. I didn't need a doctor, I needed my son back. Pat became hysterical, and begged me to go. Finally I gave in.

The doctor checked me over from head to foot, took my blood pressure, listened to my heartbeat, looked down my throat and in my ears and handed me a prescription for tranquilizers.

"You are a nervous wreck," he said.

"You're brilliant," I thought.

"The medication I ordered should do the trick. If you don't get the relief you need, don't hesitate to call me," he said, guiding me to the door.

It didn't take long before I was on the phone.

"Doc, I can't take it, I'm going crazy, I'm going out of my mind. You gotta help me."

He asked what I was using and I reminded him. Valium, Stelizine, something else. He said, "Double up on your medication." And I did.

I was going to work every day, but I wasn't earning my pay. I was hanging around with the addicts like before, but I wasn't learning anything. All I was doing was hurting.

A couple of months went by and before I knew it, it was Christmas. Christmas is a season when everything is bigger than life. It works like a magnifying glass. When you're happy, Christmas can turn your joy into ecstasy. But when you're down about as far as you can go, it's the pits. And let me tell you I was down. On Christmas Eve I passed a toy store. In the window was a little telescope that David had asked for. I went in and bought it for him. Like he would be home to receive it. Before I got home I took the toy out of its bag and smashed it against the wall of a brick building. I was nuts.

Right after that I began playing games with the tranquilizers. I didn't need a doctor or a prescription to get them. The street was a pharmacy. I didn't want to think about anything. I didn't want to know about anything. I didn't want to feel anything. I was popping more and more pills a day. Ten a day, twenty a day, thirty. Believe it or not, I built up such a tolerance for them that in a few weeks I was swallowing over a hundred tranquilizers a day. Toma, the narcotics detective, had become Toma, the narcotic addict.

I needed help, but all that was on my mind, when I was thinking at all, was that I needed relief—relief from the mental torture. I couldn't bring my son back.

I knew that. I couldn't turn back the clock to the moment he started to choke, and handle it differently. I knew that. When I let the thoughts of my son and his death into my head, it was to punish myself. That's what I deserved, I thought. It's crazy. On the one hand I wanted to be punished. On the other hand, I popped the pills because I couldn't stand the punishment.

My wife couldn't help me. She was struggling to stay sane herself. My condition made her fight for stability that much harder. She's a tough lady. It's a miracle that she didn't sink as low as I did. She couldn't help me but she tried. She pleaded with me to "go for help." That meant a psychiatrist. As far as I was concerned, shrinks were bums. They stared at you for an hour, and charged you by the minute. Sometimes, Patty lectured, reminding me of my responsibilities; how she and our kids needed me. Needed me? I had already proved that they couldn't count on me. Sometimes she'd blow up and demand that I straighten out, then I'd run upstairs and swallow a handful of pills. The rest of my family were concerned, too. My parents, my sisters and brothers.

"Look at yourself, David. Look in the mirror. You look terrible. You're getting skinny. Your cheeks are sunken. Your color . . ."

That's not what I needed. I didn't need lectures or someone demanding that I straighten out. I knew how bad I looked, I knew that I had responsibilities — I needed someone to talk to, someone who would listen and understand without judging me.

Another complication set in. Word of my behavior got to headquarters. One of my colleagues squealed on me. "Toma's losing his marbles. He's eating pills like they were peanuts," he told one of my bosses.

A police doctor was sent to my house. When I saw him coming up the walk I panicked and ran to the back of the house. I screamed to my wife, "Tell him I'm not here, PLEASE tell him I'm not here." When the doorbell rang I was in the kitchen, my body pressed against the back door. "This is it," I thought. "I've blown my job. Those bastards in the department have been trying to get rid of me. Now they can do it."

I don't know how long I stood there, trembling like a cornered rat. Pat called to me, "David, he's gone," but I couldn't move. I was frozen against the door.

Suddenly someone clutched my shoulder. I knew it wasn't my wife. I was paralyzed with fear. Pat lied! I felt myself being turned around, my eyes were squeezed shut. Then a deep voice, "Hey, what's going on, Uncle David?" When it finally sunk into my brain that this was my nephew Ronnie, that I was safe, I threw my arms around his neck and hung on for dear life. "Ronnie, help me. I'm going crazy. I'm scared. Please, help me." I began sobbing. I wanted him to put his arms around me, but he didn't.

It's ironic, isn't it. Me begging Ronnie for help. He's the nephew I mentioned earlier — the addict. When he came to me for help, I gave him a lecture. Straighten yourself up, I had told him, then I'd listen.

I don't blame him for getting in his licks. He reminded me of the times I had turned my back on him, but he wasn't looking for revenge, not even when he said, "What's the difference between you and me, Uncle David? You're strung out on your junk, I'm strung out on mine." We were at the kitchen table now. Pat slipped into the room, put some coffee on the stove and left. I don't know how long Ronnie and I talked, but it might have been hours. I did most of the yakking. Once I started I couldn't shut it off. I don't remember what was said, but I remember a feeling that began building in me. This guy cares. This punk-junkie-nephew of mine really cares. This beautiful, loving, car-

The poison I had put into my body screamed for more. And it's not easy to reject its demand.

ing boy wasn't going to let me rot in some gutter or some dingy institution.

After that, I saw Ronnie almost every day. He became my shrink and my minister and most of all, my friend. He didn't have any answers, but he listened and he cared. Gradually I clawed myself out of my hole. It wasn't easy. Plenty of times I slid back and it took everything I had to keep from falling all the way down. It took time to build up my confidence, my self-respect, to find a reason to like myself again. This was the toughest fight of my life, and I was a fighter. When I was in the Marines I was the middleweight boxing champion, but that was child's play in comparison. And when I was shot in the back and was near death, I survived because I fought for my life. This was harder. The poison I had put into my body screamed for more. And it's not easy to reject its demand.

I don't know exactly when I became addicted and I don't know exactly when I beat the addiction, but the moment Ronnie came into my kitchen and put his hand on my shoulder may have been the most important day of my life.

You can imagine how my recovery helped Patty pull herself together. I had put her through hell and she was exhausted. Thank God she was a strong woman. Our life at home gradually became normal again. The kids tested me and found out they could run through the house without having me throw a tantrum. They found out that they could talk about David without throwing me into a deep sullen mood.

I missed my lost son plenty. All of us did, but we weren't obsessed. I knew that I didn't kill David. I knew, and he knew, that I loved him. I stopped feeling guilty, at least most of the time. When a guilt pang hit me, I could handle it.

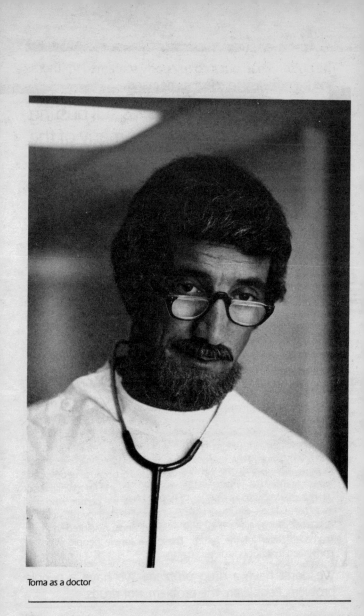

Toma as a doctor

I went back to work. I was still busting the dealers and hurting as many of the mobsters as I could, but I eased up on the small pushers. Most of them were addicts themselves, poor bastards trying to make enough bread to take care of their habit.

One thing for sure, I wasn't lecturing the kids on the street. I wasn't hassling them to straighten out and become useful members of society. They were beyond being lectured to. They were hurting and I hurt for them, but I knew that my pain wouldn't give them any relief. You can't share someone's pain with them. It's theirs exclusively. You can't suffer for them. I tried to reach out to them, tried to let them know that I was their friend, that I liked them. I wanted them to know that I knew what they were going through, that I had been there myself. Big deal. They needed more than I could give them. I couldn't give to each and every one of them what Ronnie gave to me.

Up to now everything I did to hurt the drug culture failed. First, I tried to put every user in jail. That didn't work. Then I tried to lock up every pusher and dealer. That didn't work either. Getting some of the key mob members out of circulation didn't make an impact either. You know why none of these approaches worked? We don't have addicts because drugs are easy to get. We have addicts because people can't cope with their lives; they are looking to escape, and for a while drugs and alcohol seem to be their way out. These are the people who can't deal with their families, their jobs, their teachers, their love affairs. They don't like themselves. They feel unloved and unwanted, and are scared to death of the future. These are lonely people who are convinced that nobody gives a damn.

We don't have a drug problem. We have a people problem. People are the problem, not drugs.

Toma as a hippie

It sounds so simple. All we have to do is straighten out our home lives, and our social lives; make sense out of our schools and our jobs, and start loving ourselves—and the drug dealers won't have any customers.

I had to do something. Start somewhere. I decided the place for me to start was in the schools. That's where most kids begin experimenting with drugs. Maybe I could help stop a few of them, before they scrambled their brains and were lost to the streets.

I went to one of the schools in my neighborhood, in Newark. The principal listened as I told him what had happened to me and about the addicts I saw in the streets every day I told him that if I shared these experiences with his students, maybe some of them would turn down the next joint that was offered to them. The principal said okay. He didn't think his school had a drug problem, but since I was a local cop, what the hell.

I was pretty excited the morning of my first talk. I'm not very comfortable in a shirt and tie, but wanted to show them how good an ex-addict can look. So Pat laid out my blue suit, a white shirt and maroon tie. It's a trick to make my hair behave but I did a real job on it (the dry look). I left the house looking like I was going to a wedding or a funeral. Pat reminded me to watch my language. I promised that I would.

The principal said okay. He didn't think his school had a drug problem, but since I was a local cop, what the hell.

I tell you here and now, I laid the bomb of the century. The kids that didn't split squirmed in their seats. They giggled and whispered every time I mentioned marijuana. Before I was half through, I knew that I had lost them completely.

That night I thought about my speech. What the hell went wrong? Maybe I was coming on too heavy, too serious. Maybe I needed to spice up my talk with a few jokes. "Did you hear the funny story about the little girl who was shooting up in this dingy doorway . . . ."

Who am I kidding? There's nothing funny about drugs; not even when George Carlin or Cheech and Chong are telling the jokes.

The next week I arranged to speak in another school in the neighborhood. This time a high school. I couldn't come up with any big ideas for my presentation, so I psyched myself up for another bummer. I was convinced that somebody in the audience had to be paying attention, had to be getting the message, and if I could save one child's life, etc., etc.

Friday, I was on stage in the high school auditorium, wearing my blue suit, white shirt and maroon tie and being careful not to say damn or hell. The kids were no more attentive than the group last week, but something happened this time that was different.

I was into the story of my addiction, telling them about the pain I had suffered, when a kid in the third row stood up. He was almost as big as I was and probably heavier. He cupped his hand like he was holding a marijuana cigarette, did a pantomime of gulping in the smoke, then hollered,

"Want something to put you out of your misery, fuzz?"

Then he thrust the imaginary joint toward me and the assembly howled with laughter. Other brilliant remarks could be heard through the noise, coming from different parts of the room.

The principal was on his feet, calling for quiet, but no one paid attention. The big kid was still standing, grinning and waving like a bullfighter after he made a kill. I was furious. I grabbed the microphone and roared into it.

"Sit down, you stupid asshole!" Suddenly there wasn't a sound in the room. Everyone was in his seat except the big kid. He was frozen on his feet. I lowered my voice just a little. "If you make one more sound, you chicken punk. I'll drag you on to this platform and beat the crap out of you. Here and now."

I watched the kid slump into his seat, then I took off my coat and tossed it on the floor. I loosened my tie and started talking. I was wound up. I spilled my guts to these kids. I couldn't stop. The bell rang, signalling the end of the period, but I kept on talking and the kids didn't budge.

I finally finished. I was wringing wet. I picked up my coat from the floor and turned back toward the assembly. No one had gotten up from their seats.

I said, "You may not believe this, but I love you. And I need you to love me in return . . . even the smart-ass in the third row."

The room exploded with applause.

Before I could get to the exit kids were all over the stage. They crowded around me, all talking at once. Some were crying. For the next half hour I was on the platform shaking their hands, hugging them, kissing them.

Something happened to them and to me that day.

They wanted someone to tell them that drugs are wrong! But they didn't want to be told by just anyone. They needed to get the message from someone who cared about them!

I looked into their faces and I knew with all my heart that I wasn't lying to them when I told them that I loved them.

And at that moment I knew what I wanted to do with the rest of my life.

Toma as a construction worker

Exhausted and elated, I headed for home to pick up my gear for the night's work. The news that I had spoken at the high school reached headquarters before I got there. Naturally my boss wanted to see me. If you think that he wanted to praise me, think again.

He loved telling me that before I could make another public appearance, I had to be designated as an Official Departmental Speaker.

"So designate me, sir," I said.

"No way, Toma, no way." Then he gave me a short lecture about keeping my nose clean.

I didn't argue with him. I knew that I could never change his mind about me. No use trying. It didn't matter. I knew that he couldn't keep me from doing what I had to do, on my own time.

That was in 1961, and for the next ten years I spoke on my own time and at my own expense at schools, lodges, PTA's, you name it. I never asked for money and none was ever offered. I talked in New Jersey, New York and Connecticut. Anywhere that I could get to cheaply and close enough to Newark to get home the same day.

Lots of cops take jobs on their days off, in order to supplement their salary. My part time work drove my wife half nuts, because she handled our finances and the expenses were coming out of her budget, and nothing extra was coming in.

Today I have trouble handling all the requests I get to speak in schools, but in 1961 I had trouble finding schools where I could talk. When I worked nights on my job I spent the mornings calling on or phoning school principals. I talked to them about what was happening to kids in the streets, and about all I knew of the drug dealing right

> **Cops weren't exactly the most popular people around in the sixties, and I didn't look like the kind of person who is usually invited to talk to a student body.**

in the schools. Most of them weren't interested. They wished to hell that I'd split and let them get on with their really important work. They shuffled their papers and argued that there was no drug problem in their school. They talked about the heavy load the teachers were carrying and how much confusion is caused when a special assembly is called.

I had plenty going against me. Cops weren't exactly the most popular people around in the sixties, and I didn't look like the kind of person who is usually invited to talk to a student body. And I sure as hell didn't (and still don't) sound like a speaker on the school circuit. You don't have to be a genius to figure out that Walter Cronkite and I didn't take the same speech courses.

> **Facing school administrators was a challenge, but I became pretty good at selling them. I learned to handle their objections and it wasn't long before I was talking in one or two schools a week.**

Right from the beginning I found out that most kids want to talk about their drug experiences. They are worried, they are confused. They don't know what the truth is about dope. Especially marijuana. Most of them give in to the idea that if everyone is doing it, it can't too bad. More cases are being made for it than against it. Decriminalization is a frequent topic. Isn't that the same as legalizing it? How can it be so dangerous? Their parents have a highball before dinner — so what's the big deal if they smoke a joint after school? It's the same thing, isn't it? It is not the same thing! It is nothing like the same thing. Before you finish this book, you'll know damned well what the difference is.

Right from the beginning the kids clamored for more when I finished my talk. They surrounded me on the stage and begged for private rap sessions. I would stay until the principal broke us up, or until I had to get ready to go to work. The kids wanted to talk, they wanted to share their fears without the risk of punishment or ridicule. They called me on the phone and showed up at my house after school.

34

They talked about memory lapses and their inability to concentrate. Some of them said that they couldn't understand what was being said, even when they listened. They worried about numbing sensations in their limbs and down the side of their torso. They worried and they worried. I heard horror stories that made me sick.

I came home late one afternoon and a little girl was waiting in front of my house. She was trembling and burst into tears when she saw me. In time she settled down enough to tell me her story. She was 13 years old and smoked pot only one time. She said that about three weeks before I spoke at her school she was coaxed into going to an after school party. Of course the party wasn't supervised by any adults, that wouldn't have been cool. It was held in the home of one of the students whose parents worked. They wouldn't be home until 6:30. It was innocent enough when it started—they played records and danced. Then someone brought out the grass. This little kid never tried tobacco before, let alone marijuana—but she gave into the teasing and she began to trip from the very first hit. She didn't know what was happening to her. This little 13 year old girl, who wasn't grown up enough to wear a bra, told me that between four and six o'clock that day she had sex with five different boys.

Was she a bad girl, she wanted to know. The boys wouldn't let her alone now and she was terrified. She wanted to die.

How many kids want to die? You could fill a big city with them.

How can kids who are struggling with simple relationships handle the tremendous problems that dope and alcohol create for them? You don't have to turn to Freud for the answer. They can't.

I convinced the little girl that she had to share what had happened to her with her parents, and I took her home. Her mother nearly collapsed and her father went into a rage. He was going to have the boys arrested for rape and sue the parents where the party was held for negligence. But he didn't. He pulled his daughter out of school and as quickly as he could moved to another neighborhood. His daughter may not smoke pot again, but the chances that the new neighborhood will be any different is one in a million. There's no place to run.

I spoke in every school in my area that would let me. But I was frustrated. I knew that Newark, tough as it is, didn't have a corner on the drug problem. There was no doubt in my mind that I was making an impact on the kids who heard me. I wanted to spread out. Cover a bigger area.

But I couldn't—for one thing, I couldn't afford to. I had to work to support my family, and we weren't living in luxury on my salary. Sometimes when I talk about it, I think I sound a little nuts, but I really wanted to reach more kids. I hoped that other people would be impressed with what I was doing and join the fight. But not much happened. Sometimes I would see an article where somebody was researching the effect of marijuana on rats, and the studies seemed to imply that the drug may be dangerous to people. I'd want to scream, "For crissakes come with me, talk to the kids, let them tell you what pot is doing to their heads. You don't have to screw around with rats or monkeys to find out." I wanted everybody in the world to know what I knew. But the chances were that no one outside of the Newark area was going to pay any attention to a Newark cop.

One morning I was sitting on the edge of my bed, fumbling through a stack of books Patty had piled up on her nightstand and I made a decision. I would write a book. I sprung my big idea on Patty and the kids that night at dinner. I should have known better. The kids groaned. They had listened to me rant and rave about drugs all their lives, so what's new?

Patty said, "David, let the writers write. You're helping in your own way. Between working and speaking in schools you're tied up in knots now. Please."

I should have listened to her.

I spent the next five months writing. Before work, after work, sometimes during work. By the time I was finished I had filled a stack of legal pads, written in longhand.

New York City is the publishing capital of the world and it isn't far from Newark, New Jersey. I got a copy of Manhattan's Yellow Pages and my spirits soared when I saw how many publishers were listed. In my heart I knew that one of them would publish my book. I didn't expect them to fall over themselves when I showed up, but I was confident that once I had their ear, I'd convince them. It took a long, long, long time before I allowed myself to know how wrong I was.

Newark is close to New York City all right, but I must have travelled a million miles, trying to connect with one publisher.

My wife begged me to stop. The whole neighborhood knew what I was doing and I was the joke of the century. Even my kids were embarrassed. A lot of people thought I was nuts, and maybe I was, because—are you ready for this?—I carried my manuscript to New York City once a week for five years!

For five years I listened to the same crap over and over again.

"Kids won't buy a book that puts down drugs."

"It's the inner-city kids who are messed up with drugs, and no one's concerned."

"Maybe if you were a celebrity, or a well-known M.D. or a psychiatrist . . ."

Finally, I was convinced. I heard their words all right, but I didn't believe them. I'm not saying that they were lying—they may have believed that they were right—but the message I got was this: You better know the right people, or have a lot of money, or be someone special—otherwise nobody is going to listen to you.

Patty knew long before I did that I wasn't going to get published, and she was relieved when I finally admitted it to myself. She was relieved and apprehensive at the same time. I don't take defeat very easily and I was rough to get along with. I was angry and wallowed in self-pity and self-righteousness. Patty did her best to bring me out of it. Most of all she let me know that she loved me and didn't think that I was a failure.

One day my wife said that I was pushing too much.

"David, quit pushing. Quit fighting all of the time. People can't stand to be around you. You're always on a soapbox. Live a little. Things will work themselves out."

Things will work themselves out? Baloney! Even my wife had to know that that's a crock. If you want something to happen, you have to make it happen. Problems never solve themselves. If you don't deal with them, they get worse.

"This country is in big trouble, baby, and you're going to be the ones to suffer the most."

I had an opportunity to stay home for a couple of days. What an opportunity. I was working in a rough neighborhood, dressed up in a three piece suit and carrying a doctor's valise. I was stalking a big dealer.

A couple of punks jumped me and began beating the crap out of me. They wanted the pills they thought were in the bag. They got away with the empty bag and I went home with a pain in my kidney you wouldn't believe. Anyway, I planted myself in front of the television set and for two days watched game shows and talk shows. The talk shows inspired a crazy idea. It was so off the wall that I was embarrassed to share it with Patty.

If you have to be a celebrity to be heard, then I'll try to become a celebrity. So I made a list of talk shows that originated in the east, phoned the networks and eventually found out who was in charge of each show's guest list.

Something prevented me from making the phone calls to these people. My ego. My pride took a terrific beating when I was trying to peddle my book, and I wasn't looking forward to another bout like that. I thought about an agent, but who would want to represent an unknown cop? Besides, who could sell Toma better than Toma? I figured out a way to do the job myself and protect my vanity at the same time.

I phoned the Johnny Carson show. "Hello," I said, "I'm Captain Smith with the Newark Police Department. I'm calling to tell you about this incredible cop named David Toma. Not only is he the smartest and most courageous policeman on the force but he's the world's greatest disguise artist." They weren't interested. I went through the list, using different names and different voices, without getting an audition. Then I remembered that the Mike Douglas Show originated in Philadelphia. I called them and scored. The lady in charge was terrific. We must have talked a half an hour and finally she said, "I'd like to meet your Mr. Toma. Will you have him get in touch with me?"

"Oh, I can't do that. Toma would kill me if he knew that I phoned you. He's a very modest guy. You call him, I think he's home right now. But you gotta promise not to mention my name." I gave her my phone number, hung up, and waited for her call. After about twenty minutes I began to get worried. Maybe I'd blown it. I was reaching for the phone to call again when it rang.

When she asked me to come in for an interview, I answered in disbelief. "Me? On television? You gotta be kidding. Is this some kind of a prank? Who told you about me? Who told you to call?" She wouldn't tell.

The audition went well — I demonstrated a few of my disguises, was asked a lot of questions about some of the big busts I made, and I was scheduled to appear. I got to tell you I was excited and so was my family. I knew that I wouldn't have the chance to talk about the subject that interested me the most — kids and drugs — but that was okay. When I was famous, I'd choose my subject.

The Mike Douglas show was taped and didn't appear on Newark television until three weeks later. The night of the airing my whole family showed up to watch with me, Patty and the kids.

We were all glued to the set watching me do my quick changes. Then Mike Douglas motioned for me to join him and he said, "David, now that you've exposed your secret to the world, can you still be an effective undercover detective?"

"Sure I can, there's no limit to the faces and personalities I can hide behind." I don't know what made me blurt out the next sentence, but I did. "I'll tell you what I really want, Mike. I want a television series of my own. Based on my own life."

I didn't get a chance to explain. Mike Douglas laughed and so did the audience. Then they cut away to a commercial and the next guest was announced.

Patty let out a groan. "Oh, David, how could you say such a stupid thing!"

My daughter, Donna, picked up from there and started to cry. "How am I going to face my friends? You sound like such a braggart."

One sentence changed me from a hero to a bum. As far as my family was concerned I was always putting my foot in my mouth, embarrassing them. I went to bed and stared at the ceiling in the dark. I knew that what I wanted was not crazy or stupid. And nothing that I wanted was impossible to achieve, so long as I had my health and was willing to work for it.

The next day I went to work and when I entered the locker room I was greeted by howls of laughter from my colleagues. They jumped up and down like kids at a three year old's birthday party. They chanted, "Toma is a movie star, movie star, movie star . . ." The front of my locker was covered with men's room graffiti. Another time I might have plowed into them, but this day I was drained. I just stood there.

Then one of them yelled, "You're in big trouble, Charlie Chan, the boss said to get your ass upstairs the minute you get here."

I was in trouble. I could tell it the second I entered his office. He was calm. He had a happy look on his face. He picked up a manual off his desk and started reading to me. Enjoying every word of it. In a nutshell it said that no cop can appear on television without prior consent of his superior officer. He had been waiting a long time to nail me for something. He couldn't make an issue of me talking to kids about the hazards of dope, but this was different. This time I appeared on national TV like a burlesque act.

He didn't lecture me or blow up, he didn't have to. All he said was, "Toma, gimme your gun."

He broke into a grin when I passed the weapon to him. Then he rearranged his face into its usual scowl and ordered me to see a psychiatrist.

So every day, at taxpayer's expense, I went to see the psychiatrist.

I don't know if the captain really thought that I was nuts or if he believed that I wouldn't be able to stand the humiliation, and would resign from the force. He could never believe that my appearance on the Mike Douglas Show had anything to do with drugs and kids and my deep concern for them.

At first I thought that I had gone back to kindergarten. I played with the pegboard, told the man what I saw in the ink blots, and played word games with him.

Then we got down to serious business. He dug into my childhood, trying to find out why I hated my parents.

I love my parents!

He couldn't believe that. He kept digging and probing, hell-bent on proving to me that deep down in my subconscious mind I had to hate them. He was frustrated with me, but he finally gave up on that point. I don't know what he wrote down in his notebook, but it was probably something like, "This guy Toma may be dangerous, he's got abnormal feelings about his parents."

Nobody thinks that I'm a genius. Not even my mother. I don't know what my I.Q. is but I'm sure it wouldn't get me into the Harvard Business School. I'm not an idiot either. Sometimes my zeal to accomplish what I believe in—my passion to express what I know is the truth — makes some people look at me as though I'd escaped from an institution for the criminally insane.

I told him something that made him turn pale. His eyes popped open and so did his mouth, and he began scribbling a hundred words a minute. I don't know why I confided in him, and I'm not sure why

I'm going to repeat it to you now. I may sound like an egomaniac, but I swear to you that I felt then—and still feel—that regardless of all my shortcomings, God gave me a gift, an ability to reach a troubled generation. And I am driven to use this gift, to reach these children.

Kids trust me, they accept my love, and thousands of them quit drugs after spending a single day with me. I tried to explain to the shrink what an incredible high that gave me . . . and the tremendous burden it placed on me.

Like I said, I don't know what he wrote in his notes and he never told me what he thought, but he apparently decided that I wasn't ready to be institutionalized. And about a month after my appearance on television, I was back on the job.

I almost felt sorry for my boss. He had to return my gun to me. It wasn't easy for him, he thought that he could get rid of me and he gave it his best shot. So all he could do now was give me a lecture. Warn me of the consequences if I ever pulled another Mike Douglas Show on him again.

While he was giving me the business, the phone rang. He answered it, then shoved the phone toward me.

"It's for you Toma—long distance."

"It can't be for me. I don't know any . . ."

"Take the phone," he growled. "It's Hollywood."

We stared at each other with disbelief.

Mike Douglas and his audience laughed when I said that I wanted a TV series based on my life. My wife and kids were embarrassed to tears. My colleagues treated me as though I had leprosy. But, by God, there I was—an arm's length away from the guy who had tried to put me away in a mental institution—listening to the sweet music of recognition. Recognition coming from 3000 miles away.

"You've been very difficult to reach, Mr. Toma," the voice said. "We've been trying for almost a month."

I couldn't say that I've been putting in my time on a police psychiatrist's couch.

"Sometimes my work takes me out of the country. I've been on a special assignment in the Bahamas," I lied.

My boss snorted loud enough to be heard in California without a telephone. I couldn't care less. The guy on the other end of the line was from Universal Studios and was talking about a movie of my life.

"How soon could I come to Hollywood," he wanted to know. "How fast does a plane fly?" I asked.

This would be the first time that I travelled west of New Jersey, except for my stint in the Marines. And the very first time that I would travel by air.

My family went with me to the airport to see me off. Not only my wife and kids, but my parents, Ronnie, and two of my sisters. My mother packed me a lunch! It was like I was leaving the Old Country headed for a brave new world.

The minute I stepped on the plane I began to feel like a celebrity. Not that anybody knew who I was—but I had such a strong feeling that before long they would.

As it turned out I got their attention a lot sooner than I expected or wanted.

The flight took five and a half hours and I was sick for five and a half hours. When I wasn't throwing up or on the verge of passing out, I was frozen in my seat, my hands clenched on to the armrests like steel vises. Lucky for the gentleman who was assigned to the seat next to me, there was an empty seat for him to move to.

I hate to admit it but I began to get sick while the plane was still on the ground, taxiing down the runway. Tough cop.

A little man in a chauffeur's costume met me in L.A. He picked up my bags and led me to a Mercedes-Benz limousine that was so long it took up two parking spaces. Baby, I had arrived! Toma in Hollywood. I settled into the back seat of that limo, turned on the television set, poured me a glass of orange juice from the bar that was stocked with liquor and enjoyed every second of the forty minutes it took to get to Universal.

It was a short walk from where we parked to the offices and I was all eyes. I passed Lucille Ball and Rock Hudson, Peter Falk and Burt Lancaster. And the starlets—they were giving me the eye just in case I turned out to be someone important. It was like a dream and I didn't want to wake up.

Nothing much happened at the first meeting. I met a few people and there was some talk about a feature-length film based on my life. I pushed for a TV series. I honestly felt that what I had to say could not be squeezed into an hour and fifty minute movie.

On that trip I was in Hollywood for only five days. They put me up in a suite of rooms in a fancy hotel right across from the studio, and I got to tell you I was snowed by them. But what I saw was a world that was crazier and sicker than what you find on the streets of Newark, New Jersey. Booze, drugs, depravity. It was everywhere. The characters were more sophisticated and their wardrobes a lot fancier, but the games they were playing were no different. Just sicker. I knew that I couldn't relate to these pill poppers and coke snorters as easily as I could to Newark's street junkies. But I tried to push all negative thoughts out of my mind. I was here for a purpose, and I didn't want to blow it. Eventually I would get to the kids and Hollywood would be the vehicle.

On the fourth morning the limo picked me up at the hotel and drove me to the studio. I was a little edgy. For three days I had been treated like royalty but there hadn't been any serious talks.

I felt like a yokel on a sightseeing trip. I wanted to get things moving.

The gorgeous secretary led me into the attorney's office and before she got out of the room, he said, "Is Mr. Toma's contract ready?"

Just like that! No discussions, no negotiations, no nothing.

Mr. Toma's contract was ready and a minute later the attorney shoved it under my nose.

Honest to God, I was so flattered, so dazzled, that I would have signed it without reading a word if he hadn't received an urgent phone call and had to leave the office.

By the time he returned I had gone over the contract three or four times. There was plenty that I didn't understand about it, but what I did understand nearly put me in a state of shock.

It was a nothing contract. Nothing at all. Universal had no intention of involving me in a movie or a TV series or anything else. They wanted to tie me up for the future, just in case they decided, someday, to do another cop series. They wanted to buy my name and my life story for $1000. That's why they sent for me. If they ever decided to do a show about an undercover cop in Newark they'd let me know. Goodbye Charlie.

The lawyer didn't argue with me. As far as he was concerned there was nothing to talk about.

"Take it or leave it, Mr. Toma," he said. What a choice.

I was nearly in tears. "You take it and shove it."

"My mother taught me the meaning of love. My father showed me that a parent's responsibility is forever."

When I headed for the airport—this time in a bus—I was in a state of shock. I had taken plenty of beatings in my life, but none like this.

Two pimps broke my back while another held a gun on me. I was shot in the back by a mafia soldier. I was stabbed in the chest by a drug-crazed loonie—but they didn't hurt me like Hollywood hurt me. This time my self-esteem was shattered. It was like my dignity was flushed down the toilet.

I set myself up for the hit. I did the dreaming and the fantasizing. Less than a week before, I left Newark, New Jersey, like a hero—cocky, self-assured. Now I was returning a failure, to face the people I love and a police department that didn't love me.

Somehow I blew it. It was in my fingers and I let it slip away. I let those sons-a-bitches beat me. They wanted me for a first-class ticket on an airplane, and little sweet talk and a thousand bucks. I felt like they tried to trick me into becoming a whore.

I didn't get sick on the plane going home. I was so busy trying to figure things out—what happened, what I was going to tell my family, what I would do next—that I don't remember the plane taking off or landing. But by the time the jet came to a halt I had made one decision. I would go back to Hollywood.

I didn't travel 3000 miles for someone to make an ass out of me. I went there to put together a television series, because I wanted to be heard. And I would make it happen. I kept telling myself that I am a fighter. That I'm worth whatever effort it takes to make it. That what I want to do with my life is important—and not just to me.

Thank God for Patty. Being married to me was never easy and one of the roughest times in her life followed my return from California. She knew that I had to go back. She knew that I couldn't return to work with this thing hanging over my head. Most of the sacrifice would be hers, she knew that too. But she was willing to see me through this. She loves me, she says, that's why she puts up with me. I tell her that she must have a head full of spaghetti.

After Pat and I talked it over and gave the kids a chance to sound off, I called the Department and asked for a three month leave of absence. They didn't hassle me about it, I guess they were glad to get rid of me for awhile. Next came the tough part. The money. We lived in a rented house, had three children and about $5.00 in the bank.

Patty started looking for a job and I looked for money to borrow. There was no use going to the bank, we didn't have anything to put up for collateral. So I had to go after the family. Mine and Patty's. Everyone of them came through. A few of them lectured me but only one put up a fight. My pop. I couldn't blame him, he worked his can off all of his life—two jobs most of the time. He was a frugal man who worried about the future. It was no easy thing for this Italian immigrant to dig into his life savings so his son could go chasing a dream in Hollywood. He would have held out but Mamma got on his case. And as every Italian knows, what Mamma wants, Poppa does.

I worried plenty about my kids. The oldest, Jimmy, was only ten, the youngest, Janice, had just started school and we were a very close family. Although I often worked crazy hours they knew that Daddy came home every day and went to church with them at least once a week. I promised them that no matter what happened I would phone them from California every day, and that's a promise I kept. One three minute phone call a day became an important part of our budget.

There were moments when I wasn't sure that I could go through with my plans. What if I failed when I got to Hollywoodd? How would I ever pay back the money I was borrowing? And even if I succeeded, how long would it take before any money would come in? What if Pat or one of the children got sick? What if there was an emergency and they needed me right that moment?

When it became apparent to Pat that I was having self-doubts she made a suggestion. Could I possibly arrange to take in one more school—to reinforce what I believed in—before leaving for California?

Two days on the phone and I got booked into a junior high school. The principal agreed to let me have a private room after my lecture, in case any of the kids wanted to talk to me alone. The date was set for two days before I would leave my home.

It was a suburban school, almost lily-white. The kids were attentive and polite and I could tell that they enjoyed my cop stories. But when I got into drugs more than a few became uncomfortable. Some began to fidget, hang their heads, wipe their forehead, give knowing sidelong glances to the kids around them. One girl near the front began to cry, and when she tried to wipe her tears away she smeared her eye make-up across her cheek. I wanted to cry with her.

Dear God, what is happening in this country? Must we adults sit back like television viewers and watch our children destroy themselves and each other with drugs? Are we stupid or are we mad? Is it possible that most of us don't know what's going on?

"There are kids in this room—right now—who are in deep trouble. Where are your parents—don't they know what you're doing to yourselves with drugs? Don't they give a damn about you? What about your teachers? They have to know that you're screwing around with drugs. Don't they give a damn about you? And what about you? Do you think that because your parents and teachers are looking the other way, you have the right to destroy yourselves. Have the pot and pills got your minds so messed up that you're willing to swap your lives for a chemical high?"

The girl with the streaked face was sobbing out loud. The girl in the next seat tried to calm her, but she was crying too.

I talked for another half an hour, then told the group that I was available for a private rap and gave them the room number. The kids began to file out of the auditorium, but the girl I had noticed was still in her seat. She accepted my hand and together we walked to the room that was assigned to me.

Here's what she told me: Her name was Ellen, she was 14 years old and a few days before she attempted suicide. This was her first day back in school. 14 years old and she had enough of life on earth.

Her mother split five years before and she hadn't heard from her since. It didn't matter, she said. Her father was okay. He didn't hassle her about anything, gave her a weekly allowance and didn't abuse her in any way. She imagined that he loved her but she wasn't sure. He never said and she never asked. They never had a personal conversation and she could never remember being kissed or hugged by him. She didn't hate him. She didn't think much about him . . . she didn't know him.

She began smoking pot when she was nine years old—soon after her mother left. It started in the school yard when five or six kids shared a joint. She didn't get high and she didn't get sick, but it was kind of exciting. She smoked once in a while, but not regularly, until three years later. That's when she met a 14 year old named Roy.

She didn't think much of him at first—not until he told her that he thought she was pretty. A relationship developed. She became his girl. He supplied her with The Pill and almost every day after school he came to her house and they got high on marijuana and had sex.

About a year later the boy began experimenting with other drugs. He wasn't satisfied to play with them himself, he insisted that she take them too. Uppers, downers, mostly speed. She was afraid of taking pills but he threatened to get another girl and she couldn't face that. She never belonged to anyone before—no one ever belonged to her. So she started popping pills.

Roy's personality began to change. He began getting rough with her. He stopped telling her that she was pretty. Now she was homely and dumb and good for nothing but sex.

A couple of months ago he began using heroin. This she resisted with all her might. A week ago he gave her an ultimatum—join him or he was through with her. She couldn't face either possibility.

Luckily, her girlfriend found her unconscious on the living room floor of her home. She had OD'd on pills. Ellen's father was on a business trip when this happened. He was told that she had had food poisoning and he accepted that.

What do you think Ellen had planned for that evening after my lecture? She was going to meet Roy. What difference did it matter how she died, she had decided.

She changed her plans now, and I agreed to go to her house with her and meet her father.

I spent the next three hours talking to the kids who had been waiting. More than 50 had waited, about 15% of the student body. They reinforced what I already knew. 85% of the students in the junior high were playing around with drugs—mostly pot. About 50% were smoking dope more than once a week. That is heavy pot smoking! I'll explain why later. One of the teachers in the school smoked marijuana with a few of the kids, and told these children of other teachers who used the stuff. On and on and on.

I might as well finish Ellen's story. That evening I went to her home, and listened to the 14 year old tell her story to her father. She was a brave girl, she didn't leave anything out: the drugs, the sex, the suicide attempt.

Her father stared straight ahead while she talked. No expression on his face. As if he were hypnotised.

Finally she stopped talking.

"How could this happen?" he whispered.

"Why didn't you know it was happening?" I asked.

There was a long pause then Ellen spoke.

"Daddy, do you love me?"

The man's face became twisted with pain. He let out a long sorrowful groan and burst into tears. Then he reached for Ellen and smothered her face with kisses.

"I love you, my daughter. I love you, my daughter."

Through her tears Ellen whispered, "I love you, Daddy."

For fourteen years he had been her father and she his daughter, and this was the first time either had heard those words.

What in the hell happens to us? Where are our priorities?

Ellen's in her 20's now. She's married to a nice guy and she works with troubled children. She doesn't have any of her own yet. She's afraid to become a mother. She has read all the research on drugs that's available, and she is afraid that marijuana may have damaged her reproductive system.

I can't give her any advice, because I know that it's a crapshoot.

My wife was right. The doubts that were building up in me were wiped out after just one day in that junior high school.

Patty got a nine to three job, so at least the kids would have their mother full time when they were home from school. And I'll be lucky, I told myself. I'd be home in a month or so.

I didn't travel first-class this time, a limousine wasn't waiting for me at the airport in L.A., and I didn't have a reservation for a suite of rooms in a celebrity-populated hotel. Anything but.

As soon as we landed I went to the Yellow Pages of the phone book looking for hotels that couldn't afford display ads. Then I began phoning.

"What are your weekly rates? How close are you to Universal studios?"

The best I could do was a hotel about four miles from the studio. With my bad back, walking as fast as I could, I would be able to make it to the studio in an hour and fifteen minutes.

I didn't care. There was a cheap diner close by, there was a public telephone in the lobby, and the walk to Universal wasn't too hilly.

What I hoped to accomplish made sense to me. Universal had been interested in me enough to fly me to Hollywood and try to con me into selling them my story for a thousand bucks. So I'd have to convince them that they were on the right track, but that they needed more than my name and story. They needed me.

I would have to convince them that they would be foolish to buy the idea and then file it away with thousands of other ideas that would never get out of the drawer. I wanted them to do a television series, not a one-shot movie. I wanted my name attached to the series and I wanted to have something to say about what they put on the air.

That's what I wanted.

What they wanted was for me to drop dead.

The first guy I tried to see was the attorney who tried to get my name on that contract. I sat in his outer office for almost a week before he agreed to see me.

The meeting lasted almost five minutes. Talking a mile a minute he spelled out his position in plain non-legal language.

I was wasting his time and mine, he said. Universal had completed their business with me. They own the rights to thousands of stories, not too many of which end up in a movie house.

"Go home, Mr. Toma, you must have something better to do."

I wanted to hit him. More than anything I wanted to wipe that condescending smirk off his face, but I didn't.

I didn't go home either. Instead I visited every producer, director, and studio executive that I could find. Mostly I talked to secretaries and receptionists. I became a fixture in their offices. Some mornings I would show up with coffee and donuts for the women who guarded the doors of the movie monarchs. I became friendly with most of them, but it wasn't opening any doors for me.

Every night I called home and talked to Patty and the kids. My wife always sounded cheerful. Everything was great. I knew she was lying. I pretended that things were really moving. The break would come any minute. She knew that I was lying.

Almost two and a half months passed and I was no closer to putting a deal together than I was the day I arrived.

It began to sink into my thick skull that there was a real possibility that Hollywood was going to beat me again. I had to psych myself up every morning to take that four mile walk. My back was killing me; almost every step I took was painful. All the injuries suffered on the job were taking their toll. Even worse than the morning walk was the hike back to the hotel in the evening. Nothing accomplished.

Every time I spent a dollar, I wondered who worked for that buck. My Pop? My sister? My brother-in-law? I began to feel that I had conned them, the way the studio had conned me.

One evening something happened. The night clerk at the hotel had a message for me. The slip of paper had a name and a phone number on it. The name belonged to the secretary of one of Universal's top TV producers. I knew that the area code wasn't Universal's, so I figured she was calling me from home.

"Maybe she's feeling sorry for me and is going to invite me to her house for dinner." I said this to the night clerk, but he had his face buried in a porno magazine and wasn't paying any attention.

Well, she didn't offer to feed me, but she had talked to her boss about me. He was interested.

"He'll see you tomorrow morning. Ten o'clock," she said.

All night long I kept thinking, "This is my last shot. If I blow it this time, I'm a goner." I made up my mind that I'd listen, not push too hard, no matter what keep my cool.

He was thirty minutes late for the appointment and I was thirty minutes early, but that was all right. He was amiable enough when he finally showed and we settled down in his Hollywood set office.

He asked me a million questions about my experiences as an under-cover cop. And I told him story after story —everything that happened to me from the time I joined the police force until I came to Hollywood.

He was interested, no doubt about it.

More than anything I wanted him to be impressed with my work in the schools. I hoped that he would be shocked and outraged by the epidemic of drug addiction and alcoholism that was weakening a whole generation of our children. But he seemed only mildly interested in that part of my story. What really excited him was my battle in the streets with the hard-core criminal.

I had decided the night before not to push and I was determined to stick to that. All I wanted was a commitment from him. Once a series was underway, I knew that he'd agree to covering that part of my life.

Nothing was settled that day, but Patty knew that I was telling the truth that evening when I told her that important things were beginning to happen.

We met three or four times during the next few days. Sometimes alone, sometimes with members of his staff. Mostly writers. More questions, more stories.

Then on a Friday, late in the afternoon, he said it.

"Okay, David, we'll make a pilot."

I was almost in tears—I had worked so damned hard and long to hear those words.

"If we're lucky, the network will go for it. We're going to give it our best shot—topnotch writers and a first-rate actor to play the lead . . ."

He warned me not to get too excited. More pilots were shot down by the networks than picked up by them, he said.

"No way, baby," I thought. "No one would shoot down this show."

Then came the icing on the cake. He wanted me to stay on as story consultant. And "it might be a great gimmick if you appeared in each episode in a different role." And as far as he was concerned, TOMA would be a good name for the series.

I had to hang on to the chair I was sitting in for fear that I'd float right out of the office. I did it. I mean I really did it! This time Hollywood didn't beat me, I beat it.

I was so high that when he got around to talking about money it seemed like a voice was coming from a million miles away. He explained the economics of producing a pilot. The cost, the risk, the fact that most of them ended up in the garbage can.

I heard him okay, but I wasn't going to let any negative thoughts ruin that moment—at least for a little while.

When I came down off my high I realized that I had gotten myself into a big League crapgame with a lot of high rollers and I was the only one playing who couldn't afford to lose.

TV pilots are a gamble. No money is made until a network buys the show, and that can take a lot of time.

I was in no position to talk the studio into paying me much front money. I was lucky to get enough to cover my expenses in Hollywood, but not enough to send any money home to Patty and the kids.

When I phoned her with the "good news" she tried to be supportive, but it was almost impossible.

"I know you have to do this," she said, "but the money we borrowed is almost gone. We can't ask for any more. How are we going to pay the rent? How long will it take until the series is sold?"

I didn't know.

All I knew was that I had to see this through. Our whole future was on the line.

I knew that I couldn't stay on the police force much longer. Not that I would be forced out by my superiors, although they would never stop trying. But my body had taken a terrific beating. I was always in pain. I had been hospitalized 32 times because of wounds and injuries that I received while on duty. I couldn't take much more.

No way could I hack it as a desk cop. I was never a team player, could never become part of the system.

The truth is all I wanted to do was work with kids. What I had been doing part time, free for ten years, I wanted to do full time. And I needed to be paid enough to support my wife and kids.

I knew in my heart that no one would pay an unknown cop to speak in a public school. I had to become a celebrity, no matter what it cost me. The time and the financial sacrifice would be the cost of getting my credentials. Like getting a college degree.

The only solution was unbearably painful. We would have to give up our home, and Patty and the children would have to move in with my mother and father.

We had no other choice. We would have no money to pay the rent. My father was furious. How could a Toma do this to his woman and their children? Thank God I didn't have to face him and try to make him understand. Thank God my mother understood. Mostly, thank God for Patty.

Tony Musante was selected to play the role of Toma and they couldn't have picked a better actor. He was terrific.

Susan Strasberg played Patty's part. The studio picked up the tab to fly my wife and kids out for a couple of weeks, so that the actors could get to know them and get a feel for their roles. It was their only trip to Hollywood.

The pilot for the series was completed and ready to be presented to the networks when one of the executives came up with the idea of changing the name from Toma to Super Cop. I hated it and fought like hell.

"Toma has to be a man first and cop second," I argued. "I want every kid who sees the show to know that ordinary people can do extraordinary things, if they really care about life. Their own, and others."

It was one argument that I won. Toma would be the name.

ABC picked up the series and it was a hit. Musante was terrific and it looked like the show could run forever. But it didn't.

After a year, Tony announced that he was quitting. He wanted to do other things. He didn't want to be a one character actor. I couldn't blame him for that.

The studio searched for a replacement and came up with Robert Blake.

I can't argue about his acting ability, but I didn't like him. His philosophy of life and mine are millions of miles apart.

His ideas about the show were different than mine. He didn't want to be a family man, he wanted a bird instead of kids. He wanted more violence. I never fired my gun at anyone. He couldn't see that. How can you have a cop show without the hero killing bad guys?

Now I was all for changing the name of the show from Toma to Baretta. Although the stories were based on my experiences and I was retained as Story Consultant, the character strayed from what I'm all about. I never smoked a cigarette in my life and I never tasted a drink that contained alcohol and I was as tough as anyone. I proved that you didn't need any chemical stimulants to be a man. I wanted that kind of person portrayed on the tube, but Blake was the star and that was one argument I couldn't win.

I wasn't a big movie star, but the name Toma was now known world wide. Not like Sinatra or Coca-Cola but enough that national magazines like Time and Newsweek did stories about me, and talk shows were happy to have me as a guest.

Three books called Toma were published. One hardcover, two in paperback.

For whatever reason, there was interest in the man behind Musante's Toma and Blake's Baretta.

And I loved it. I ate it up. I enjoyed signing autographs and it tickled me when superstars and Hollywood bigwigs called me by my first name.

I gotta tell you, I was "going Hollywood." If it wasn't for my wife I'd have gone completely bananas.

She hated Hollywood. She didn't like what it was doing to me. Patty is a private person and she never for a minute forgot who she was or what her priorities were. She fought to keep us "normal".

She refused to move our family to the west coast. She didn't want our kids to become Hollywood brats.

And she wasn't about to give up her lifelong friends for my new ones.

So I commuted from coast to coast, flying back and forth every couple of weeks.

I almost forgot why I went to Hollywood in the first place. I hate to admit it, but I almost forgot the kids in the schools and my fight against drugs.

Of all the episodes we did, only one carried a really stong antidrug message that would touch the kids. That one was based on an incident when one of my nephews overdosed on heroin. Incidentally, that show drew more mail than any other.

Then one day a booking agent phoned me.

"Mr. Toma," he said, "would you consider doing a lecture tour? . . .I've seen you on television and I think that with a little coaching you could be a dynamite speaker."

With a little coaching? Come on, man, I talked on stage for ten years and never put anyone to sleep.

"What kind of engagements do you have in mind?"

"College campuses."

He told me the names of some of the colleges he could line up and how much money they would pay. I thought he was putting me on. He was talking big money for 90 minute lectures.

This was perfect! I was fed up with the way the show was going. I could be home three or four days every week, and Patty and the kids would be overjoyed.

"But David, why colleges? Why not the schools?" Patty asked.

I told her what the agent told me. There was no school "market" for speakers. They had no money for lectures, even if they wanted them.

They had no facilities to handle the kind of audiences that a college could turn out.

Besides, who ever heard of a "celebrity" talking in a junior high?

I was doing okay financially now. Retired from the police force—moved into a lovely home in a small New Jersey town—paid off all our debts—and bought a couple of luxury cars.

We were doing fine, but I still had a wife and four kids to support and I was in no position to travel the country at my own expense, giving free lectures.

And I have to admit that I couldn't go from the glitter of Hollywood back to the small auditoriums and gyms with their makeshift sound systems and their impossible acoustics.

You got it figured out—my head had gotten as big as an elephant's.

For ten years I busted my butt to talk in schools. Anywhere that I could get to, to any group who would listen to me. I was willing to do almost anything for the privilege of talking to kids — and it never occurred to me to ask for money. The high I got when a kid emptied his pockets of drugs and said, "I quit" was the greatest payment I could ask for. But after a couple of years in Hollywood, that experience seemed light years ago.

So I met with the agent and we talked big business. Percentages, expenses, travel accommodations, publicity and advertising. I signed a contract.

It was okay. Doing colleges, I mean. Sometimes the crowd was huge. Some over 20,000 people. And it was easy. I'd get into town in the middle of the afternoon—rap with a few professors and the press, and go on stage at 8 o'clock. Ninety minutes later, I was finished and either headed to the next campus or home. Beautiful.

It's a different ballgame today. I have to arrive in the area the night before I go to work in a high school or junior high, because my program starts at 9 A.M. Kids are bused in from other schools. I talk to the students and staff for about two and a half hours—then I ask the adults to leave and talk to the kids alone for another half hour or so. The next four hours I meet with small groups of students or with individuals who want private conferences. About 4 or 4:30, I take a break. I have what is usually my only meal of the day, and lie down for an hour or so. Try to unwind. At 7 or 7:30, I'm on stage again. Usually in a larger facility—this time talking to the parents and their children. The session lasts close to three hours, and is followed by a couple of hours talking with families or kids who weren't able to see me during the afternoon meetings.

One school date—14 to 16 hours. Doing colleges was like stealing money.

So why did I quit and go back to the schools? I wish I could say that it was my idea, but it wasn't.

I knew in my heart that I wasn't doing the kind of job in the colleges that I did in the schools before I went to Hollywood. I was entertaining and maybe I was provocative, but I wasn't touching the kids the way I used to—and they weren't touching me the same way either.

I knew all this, but I didn't deal with it. I managed not to think about it. I needed somebody to kick me in the butt and turn me around. I got what I needed—from Momma.

My Mother never saw me work on stage, but she was so proud when I first started talking in the schools. She could relate to what I was doing then. It was something like she did for years, in mental hospitals, prisons, old age homes, orphanages.

Well, one day the networks ran a segment that covered a speech I made in a Washington, D.C. college. I knew that my parents always watched the evening news, so I phoned them. Momma answered the phone.

"Momma, did you see me on television tonight?" I asked.

"I saw you. Poppa had it on." She didn't sound too happy.

"Well? What did you think?"

"What do I think? You're a bigshot, that's what I think."

When an Italian mother calls her son a bigshot, she makes him feel like a worm.

"Okay, Ma, what's bothering you?"

She told me.

For years I had preached that the only way to solve the drug problem was to stop the children before they got so deep in it that they couldn't get out. "What's different now?" she wanted to know, "Is money the difference?" She went on and on.

"You don't have to be such a bigshot. Who are you impressing? Not me. If someone had reached your nephews when they were eleven, they wouldn't be addicts today."

Later I called my agent in Beverly Hills.

When I told him what I wanted to do, he said, "Dave, why do you want to fool around with elementary and high schools 14 to 16 hours a day when you can make double that amount talking in colleges for one hour a night?

"If you work in the schools, you work for nothing, and do you know what 10% of nothing is? I got overhead . . ."

He was right, of course. Why should he work for pennies? But, for me, Ma was right! She put me back on track, and I've been in the schools ever since.

PART 2

WHY MARIJUANA IS THE MOST DANGEROUS, UNPREDICTABLE AND MISUNDERSTOOD DRUG

That's enough of the David Toma Story. You know who I am, where I'm coming from and the events that drove me to write this book.

Some of you may have decided that I'm an egotistical, self-serving rip-off artist who's trying to get rich by attacking what's becoming America's number one pastime. If you think that, then I'm going to have a hell of a time reaching you. You can throw this book in the garbage, because from here on, I'm going to do everything I can to interfere with your lives. I mean you kids, you parents, you teachers.

If you're playing around with drugs today, or if your friends are pressuring you to start, you better pay attention to what I have to say. If you have any dreams about your future, if you believe you have a future, you better care about what I'm going to tell you. It doesn't matter how smart you are, how high your I.Q. is, how well adjusted you are today. You better listen.

You parents, if you have children of school age, the odds are overwhelming that they are experimenting with drugs now, or soon will be. The numbers are astronomical. 85% of kids over ten years old experiment with drugs. By the time a child's in the seventh grade the odds are good that he's gone beyond the experimental stage, and is now a regular user. If you think that it's impossible that your child is in the wrong side of that statistic, then you're living with your head in the sand. You better check your health insurance policy and make sure that your kids are covered for psychiatric care, because you don't have enough money to keep your child in a mental hospital! That's where tens of thousands of them are going to end up because most kids aren't living on the outskirts of the drug culture, they are active participants in that drug culture. And they spend a good part of their day in the capital of the drug society. The school. Any school. Elementary, junior high, high. It doesn't matter if it's private, public, or parochial. When you send your child off to school in the morning, you better know that it almost is certain that you're sending them off to a drug supermarket!

I'm in a different school almost every day of the school year, and I haven't found a single school yet where drugs aren't bought and sold. The action takes place everywhere. In the playground, in the john, in the locker room—it's as easy as getting a drink of water.

In some areas the dealing is so open that the transactions are made on the streets in front of the schools. Almost any morning you can see the punk dealers, supplying the school's student pushers.

So please listen to what I'm saying, and then get together with other parents and teachers and school administrators and law enforcement agencies—and make this problem your number one priority.

Listen to what I have to say, then embrace your children—let them know that you love them no matter what—and promise to help them fight off this madness that's destroying a whole generation.

And you teachers, when you chose your profession you were pretty idealistic about it. You cared. Do you still care? Or has the system beaten you to the point where all you want to do is get through the day with as little hassle as possible. You know what's going on in your school. You know more than the administrators do. You know who the drug users are and you probably know who the pushers are. But what are you doing about it? Look the other way? Maybe you don't know what to do about it—or maybe, like most people, you underestimate the long-term effect dope can have on your students. Please hang in there with me. What you think and what you do can be the difference between sanity and insanity for a lot of kids. It can be the difference between their living or dying.

Most teachers are good, hard-working people, like most of the rest of us. Unfortunately, like the rest of us, they shrug off other people's problems. They found out that they can't change the world, so why bother to try?

Sadly, most parents think that teachers are something special. They trust them. They feel safe when their kids are under the teachers' caring supervision.

Well, I'm telling every parent, here and now, don't trust anyone to care for or protect your children. Your children are your responsibility — 24 hours a day — and you can't expect anyone to share that responsibility with you.

The teacher probably doesn't know any more about drugs than you do. And the ideas of those teachers who grew up in the sixties are probably as screwed up as anybody's. Especially when it comes to marijuana.

You can lay odds that there are teachers in your child's school who use drugs.

You can lay odds that some of them smoke dope with their students.

In almost every school that I visit, some students tell me that it was a teacher who introduced them to drugs. These teachers don't know what they are doing. The marijuana they smoke is affecting their brains! Inhibiting their ability to make sound judgments.

And what about the teachers who are clean—and that is most of them. What will he or she do if your kid comes to class stoned. Will that teacher phone you? Will he go to the principal or the school nurse? Almost never! That teacher will probably go about his business as though your child doesn't exist.

After a recent talk in a junior high school, I asked the faculty and staff to leave the auditorium (as I always do) so I could rap with the kids alone. Later I took a 15 minute break before the private sessions—one on one—would begin. I was taken to the faculty room and there I shared with a few teachers some of the things that their students had just told me.

The kids could buy any kind of drug that they wanted, right in the school building. From grass to Quaaludes to heroin.

The dealers operated out of the students' favorite hangout, which was located right across the street from the school.

Two policemen, who worked in the area, peddled drugs to the kids.

At least a half dozen teachers were known drug users, and a couple had smoked pot with some of the kids.

Kids often came to class stoned out of their minds.

Every one of the teachers seemed surprised that the students shared so much information with me, but I had the feeling I wasn't telling them anything they didn't already know.

I turned to one teacher, a young man, and asked him if any of this was new to him.

He shook his head, "no."

I went through the list. Each time I asked him, "Did you know that?" Each time he nodded, "yes."

He knew, like most of them knew, but he never said anything about it, he never did anything about it.

"Why not?" I asked him.

He looked at me, for the first time—then he dropped his eyes and shrugged his shoulders. He didn't give a damn.

The principal of this school was against me talking to his students. He was convinced there was no drug problem in his school. He was argued down by a group of parents who were just as convinced that there was a serious problem. Those few parents raised the money to bring me in by soliciting donations from several local businesses.

He couldn't believe what he saw and heard. For the first time his eyes were opened. By noon he was stunned, and by evening he was visibly shaken.

"How could all this be going on without my knowing it?" he asked more than once.

It seems incredible that he didn't know. The kids didn't tell him. And the teachers sure as hell didn't bother making waves. And when a couple of parents suspected that the school was a center for drugs and approached him about it, he shut them off. Such a thing couldn't happen in his school.

Parents have to accept the responsibility for their children. They can't count on anyone else to do the job for them.

In one midwestern state's capital, teachers and principals were interviewed by a team of newspaper reporters. They wanted to get their attitudes about drug use in the schools. Here are a few of the quotes that were published in the evening paper.

A high school teacher: "If a student is high and just puts his head on the desk, I let him be."

Does that teacher give a damn about his students? So long as the kid isn't disruptive, everything's cool. Even if he's stoned out of his head.

A high school principal: "You don't have as many kids overdosing because they are more sophisticated about drugs."

A few weeks later, six of his students were rushed to the hospital—overdosed on sopors and diet pills!

Same city, another high school principal. Here's what he tells his students, "If you must get high, do it before 7:30 A.M. or after 2:30 P.M."

I'm telling you parents right now, if you care about your kids' future, you better learn what drugs are all about. You better learn fast. And you better get actively involved in finding a solution to this deadly epidemic.

"Most of the kids in this room are playing around with drugs."

While psychologists and social scientists try to create "theories" to explain the reasons for our drug use, the physical scientists will spend the next 30 years looking into their microscopes and fiddling with their rhesus monkeys to make sure that they don't "prematurely" condemn any of the drugs the kids are using.

In the meantime, the epidemic grows. In the meantime the kids are dying! They can't learn, or grow up! In the meantime, more kids become mental, emotional, and physical cripples!

We don't have to wait three decades to condemn marijuana. We don't have to wait for the monkeys and the lab rats to tell us that grass screws up their heads!

The kids are telling us right now! The kids are telling us everything we have to know, and we are out of our minds if we don't listen to them!

We don't have 30 years to waste. We can't abandon a major portion of a whole generation and let them go to hell while the scientists work in their germ-free laboratory and the statisticians program their computers.

The research is right in front of our faces. In the schools, in the mental institutions, in the prisons. There is no reason for us to wait.

Gallup surveys a few hundred voters and tell us where this country is going politically. We accept that.

Nielsen monitors a handful of TV viewers and tells us what programs 200,000,000 people are watching. We buy that too.

I talk to tens of thousands of school kids every year, and they tell me what's happening in their schools and in their homes and in their heads.

The school is my laboratory, and the kids tell me a hell of a lot more than the monkeys and the mice tell the researchers.

You better believe it—the children are in trouble. If you accept only half of what I say, you have to believe that the children are in trouble. Believe less than half—but you must believe that the children are in trouble.

They are killing themselves with that garbage! Ruining their lives! Let's help them stop using drugs now!

The nonsense they've been told because of ignorance or greed, must be disposed of, once and for all, like garbage.

Kids will quit drugs if they know the truth about them, and if they have the support to help them quit.

I have hundreds of thousands of letters from kids who have quit—so I know what I'm talking about.

If we can curtail the use of marijuana and alcohol, we won't have to worry so much about heroin, acid, and the rest of the shit our children are taking into their bodies.

In the next chapter I am going to tell you the absolute truth about the most misunderstood drug on the street. Marijuana.

Harmless? Like taking a drink? No way brother!

Marijuana is one of the most destructive drugs around—and it's the one most responsible for wrecking the kids' minds today.

Marijuana is the most popular drug in America today, and kids are the biggest users.

It's cheaper than most of the junk that's being peddled today. It's easy to use. Lighting up isn't as scary and ugly as putting a needle into your arm. Pot parties, like booze parties, are friendly, social, ritualistic. You don't click glasses and make a toast, but you suck on a reefer, gulp in the smoke, and pass it on to the next person. That's friendly. People don't usually get mean and aggressive when they're on a marijuana high. The buzz comes fast. And there's no "hangover" afterward.

So what's the big deal about it? You just light it up like you would a Chesterfield. Inhale the sweet-smelling smoke, and exhale it out of your system. That is all there is to it.

Like hell that's all there is to it.

Marijuana contains one of the most destructive chemicals found in any drug . . . and it doesn't leave your body when you blow the smoke out of your lungs. The technical term for it is delta-9-tetrahydrocannabind. You may know it as THC. More about THC in a minute.

Before you put a match to the joint you're about to smoke, there are close to 100 different chemicals in the marijuana. More than any other drug contains. None of them belong in your body. They're poison! To make matters worse, the number of chemicals in that joint increases when you light it. Get this. The marijuana smoke you inhale is transporting more than 400 different poisons into your body. We don't even know all the damage those chemicals are doing, but we know enough to scare the hell out of us.

71

Of all the junk in marijuana, only one chemical produces the high you're paying for. That's the THC. The rest of the poison is a bonus. If marijuana didn't contain THC, no one would buy it.

When people say that pot is less dangerous than alcohol it's because they don't know about THC. They don't know what the hell they are talking about.

Alcohol is water soluble. THC is fat soluble. That's a big difference. When you drink a beer or a whiskey or any booze, your body gets rid of the alcohol in a matter of hours. You get rid of it in your urine and your perspiration. But not THC. It doesn't dissolve in water, it dissolves in fat. As soon as it gets into the body it heads for the fatty tissue—and enters the fat cells. THC gets locked into the cells of your brain, your liver, your kidneys, your glands, and in your reproductive system. Unlike alcohol, it isn't flushed out of your system in six hours. Not this poison. The THC from one joint stays in your body from three weeks to four months! And if you think it's lying there benignly, think again. That poison is playing hell with your brain, your organs, your glands, your reproductive system.

Unless you're smoking less than one marijuana cigarette every six or seven weeks the THC is accumulating in your brain and the other parts of your body. If you're smoking pot once a month the chances are that you're never free of the drug.

Do you get that? This drug is so potent that if you use it just once a month you have an active, poisonous chemical operating in your body 24 hours a day. And, my friends, if you're smoking one joint a week you are a heavy drug user. You are getting yourself into deep, deep trouble. What will the THC do to you? It will destroy your memory. It will destroy your ability to learn, to comprehend. You won't be able to follow a complex idea and you won't be able to communicate a complex thought.

Your memory will be one of the first things to go. Kids tell me every day that it gets so bad that they don't remember their phone number and address.

Educators worry because their students can't read. Kids are graduating from high school with grammar school vocabularies. Books like Why Johnny Can't Read have become best sellers, and can you believe this? College textbooks are now being written at a junior high school vocabulary level! Some people blame the problem on television. The tube is keeping youngsters away from their books, they say, they are picture oriented. Some blame it on the methods of teaching reading. There may be some truth in both of those reasons, but I guarantee you this: the THC in marijuana is screwing up the ability to learn of more than half the kids in the classroom today.

Pot does more than just that. It can mess up your speech, damage your heart and lungs and liver. It can lay a heavy dose of cancer-causing hydrocarbons on you. Do you know that there's more tar in one joint than in a carton of regular cigarettes?

And thousands of kids have told me that from marijuana alone they experience numbness in various parts of their bodies. Sometimes it lasts for a few days, sometimes for months and some say it never left them!

One of the most cruel things that pot can do is destroy the lives of children who never had the chance to say "no" to the drug. I'm talking about the offspring of marijuana smoking parents. The pot that a girl is smoking today is affecting her reproductive organs. It can affect the chromosomes and genes that she will pass on to her baby.

Have you ever seen a deformed, demented baby born of one of these mothers?

I've seen plenty of them, and it can tear your heart out. And let me tell you something else. It's not just the mother who is responsible. The mother may have never smoked marijuana. The father can cause the damage.

And when the pot-sickness gets so bad that you can't get through the day without being high, then the idea of suicide begins creeping into your mind. Kids tell me every day that suicide becomes an obsession with them. Why in the hell do you think that teenage suicide is reaching epidemic proportions?

Does it sound like we're talking about an innocent, fun drug? No way, baby. We're talking about a killer — a slow-acting, insidious murderer. Grass, reefer, tea, mary jane, weed, pot. America's favorite drug has maybe fifty pet names, but it doesn't matter what you call it— if you're fooling around with marijuana, you're putting your life on the line.

I am not telling you that every pot smoker is going to end up in a mental hospital or become parents of deformed children or will commit suicide. But plenty will. The odds against you are frighteningly high. I am telling you that every pot smoker is going to pay. Listen to this: If you smoke marijuana, you'll never reach the level of achievement that you are capable of if you don't smoke marijuana. Do you understand that? Marijuana slows down mental, intellectual, and emotional growth. It interferes with your ability to solve problems, have insights, understand relationships.

What good are you if you lose these vital abilities?

What I'm telling you now, I've been saying for almost 20 years. There was no research to support these statements then. I began talking about the effect of marijuana on the brain five years before a scientist in Israel discovered the existence of THC. How did I know? The kids who smoked pot told me. In every school I visited, I heard story after story of memory loss. Of loss of concentration and comprehension. They told me how they couldn't sustain a relationship, how they became detached from their families and close friends. How they lost their ambition and their will to achieve. But there was no serious research. No one was listening to the kids.

Dr. Ben Center, one of the most distinguished men in the field of learning disabilities, got an inkling of what was going on as early as 1961 or 1962. He conducted a class at Otterbein College for students who were flunking out of school. Among the kids who were required by the school to attend his class were a number of marijuana smokers. Many were excellent students in high school. They began smoking dope in the twelfth grade or when they were freshmen in college. Their grades began dropping by the time they were sophomores and they were flunking out of school in the junior year. They all suffered from lack of concentration, inability to remember and retain information. They couldn't solve problems. Also they were less mature than the non-pot smokers. Less mature emotionally, that is. Less responsible to themselves and to others.

"If you play, you gotta pay!"

"One of the things that was demonstrated," Dr. Center told me, "was that these students were expressing their emotions through pot-smoking, not through coping behavior." When in the hell will these kids get a chance to learn how to live? How can they survive if they can't even relate to the world around them?

I get a lot of mail from kids. I talk to a lot of them—sometimes as many as 30,000 in a week. So it's not surprising that I hear from a lot of them. I cherish this mail and save every letter. Most of the kids write to tell me that they quit dope, how long they've been clean, and how their lives have improved. Some cry for help. They're frightened and don't know who to talk to. Every now and then I get a different kind of letter, one that makes me so angry that I want to punch somebody.

A couple of weeks ago a TV producer visited my home. While he was there, my son returned from the post office and dumped about 500 letters on the floor in front of us. I told the producer to open and read as many as he wanted. The first one he picked up turned out to be one of those that make me climb the walls.

It was from a 16 year old girl from a small New England town. It started off fine. She hadn't smoked a joint since I visited the school three weeks before. She had not only been a marijuana user, she was also the top pusher in the school. When she told her dealer that she was out of the business, he exploded and "beat the shit out of me." He did a number on her that kept her out of school a few days but she was satisfied. She had paid her dues. She expected it. What she didn't expect came from her sociology teacher, the day after my appearance. My visit became the topic for the day. When several of the kids, including this girl, announced in his class that they would never smoke pot again, he burst out laughing.

"I don't believe it," he said, "he conned you. He's a phony. He doesn't know what he's talking about." He told the kids that he'd smoked pot when he was in high school and in college, and so did his friends and not one of them suffered from it.

A lot of people worked their butts off for over a year to bring me to that school. They had bake sales, paper drives, knocked on doors for donations, and other things. The kids and their parents, the teachers and the school administration really responded. An anti-drug follow-up program was established involving the whole community—and this jerko teacher tried to sabotage the effort.

Well, let me tell you something that that teacher doesn't know. He should have known because he was supposed to have attended my lecture. The pot that was smoked in the 60's ain't the same pot that is being smoked today. In comparison it was like smoking cornsilk. The THC content of the pot of the 60's was less than .02%. The THC content of the marijuana that is being smoked today runs about 6%. And there's stuff out there that has a THC content of 10% and more. So one 6% joint contains as much THC as 300 joints when that teacher was in school: If that man had smoked a joint a day for four years, he would not have sucked into his lungs as much THC as some of his students were getting in a day or two. And this guy told his students— "you got nothing to worry about. Toma doesn't know what he's talking about. He's just trying to scare you."

Well, you can bet your life that I'm trying to scare you, because I do know what I'm talking about. A teacher like this should be fired immediately.

Until a few years ago, most of the marijuana used in the United States was home grown and produced from wild seed. There weren't many heavy users because the stuff didn't have much of a kick to it. A person could get high on beer just as easily. Besides you really had to go out and look for it and it wasn't worth the trouble. For some reason it became kind of an "in" thing among some groups of jazz musicians. But its use wasn't widespread. It appeared on college campuses, but it was a novelty. There was almost nóne of it in the high schools, and none in the lower grades.

It wasn't until the early 1970's that they began to cultivate marijuana. The growers discovered that with the proper care and nurturing they were able to produce a plant that delivered a quick effective high. This didn't happen in the United States, it started in Colombia.

It didn't take long for the drug dealers in this country to find out that they had a new product that would outsell heroin and hashish. At first, smuggling the stuff was casual and amateurish. But as the market grew the distribution system became more sophisticated. Until today it is one of the slickest operations in our country, and one of the biggest industries in the world.

Every year, the quality of the marijuana improves. That is, the level of the THC increases, guaranteeing higher highs. Guaranteeing more damage to the user. But even with all the care the growers take with their crop, marijuana is unpredictable. The plant isn't consistent in the amount of THC it delivers. One plant can contain up to 60 times as much THC as the plant growing next to it. Two joints made from the leaves of a single plant may have vastly different quantities of THC.

Everything affects the plant. The sun, the shade, the water, the soil. And you can't tell by looking, feeling or smelling. And you don't know which one of the joints that you may be carrying in your pocket or your purse has the power to blow you away.

I told you that I had four nephews who became drug addicts. Let me tell you what pot did to one of them. Anthony.

Anthony started smoking pot when he was eleven years old. By the time he was fourteen he became a pusher. He had to.

It was the only way that he could keep himself supplied. By the time he was seventeen he had been arrested 105 times. But that's another story. One day a dealer sold him some really great stuff from Mexico. He shared one joint with two of his buddies. It was the best high ever. After two or three hits, Anthony felt a numbing sensation under his right arm. Then it spread down his right side. By the time the other two boys came off their high, the right side of Anthony's head began tingling, like it had fallen asleep. The sensation wouldn't go away, he felt like his head was detached from his body. After a few hours, the kids got worried and took Anthony home. By the time they got him there he was completely berserk. He raced through the house screaming in agony, knocking over tables and lamps. One of my nieces phoned me, I don't remember which one. I could hear the racket behind her as she shouted into the phone, "Uncle David, quick. Come over quick!"

The house looked like a cyclone had hit it, but when I arrived there wasn't a sound. Like the storm was over. My sister's kids were huddled in the kitchen, and my sister and Anthony's two friends were at the bottom of the stairs that go to the second floor. My sister whispered, "I think he's in his room." The two boys followed me up the stairs. Anthony's bedroom door was closed. It was quiet. Maybe he'd passed out. Just as I reached for the doorknob there was an agonizing scream and the crash of glass. I pushed open the door and Anthony, across the room, spun around and faced me. Blood was spurting from his wrist. The shattered window was behind him. We stared at each other for a moment, then Anthony moved toward a corner of the room. He crouched there, frozen, like a terrified, wounded animal.

I signalled for the boys to stay in the hall, and I started talking. "Hey, Anthony, it's me, Uncle David. Don't you recognize me?" He didn't move a muscle, but his eyes never rested. They darted from side to side, like he was looking for a way to escape. I spread my arms inviting him to come to me. He didn't budge, and I began inching my way toward him. I kept talking and shuffling toward him. When I got an arm's length away, he let out a howl and sprung at me, his bloody fist crashed against my jaw. He rushed past me toward the door, but his buddies had it blocked.

The three of us wrestled him to the floor and dragged him down the stairs, out of the house and into the car. We had to get him to the hospital. It took all three of us to keep him in the back seat of the car. My sister drove. Somehow I managed to twist my handkerchief around his arm. It slowed up the bleeding but didn't stop it. It was only a few blocks to the hospital, but it seemed like it was taking hours.

Once we got him into the emergency room the medics took over. It wasn't easy: he was wild with fear. The doctor finally got a heavy dose of tranquilizer in him and he passed out. His hand was broken and I later found out my cheekbone was fractured. I guess both breaks happened at the same time.

We all relaxed a little. The boys made little, nervous jokes about Anthony's bad trip. "Powerful shit," they kept saying. I prayed that when he woke up, the nightmare would be over.

I don't know how long he was out. Hours maybe. My sister and I were standing over him when he began to stir. When his eyes opened my heart sank. I knew that he hadn't wakened out of his nightmare. His eyes darted from side to side. He banged the butt of his good hand against the side of his head. Suddenly he let out a bloodcurdling scream. His mother fainted.

Anthony has not come out of his nightmare yet. He's been in and out of mental institutions for almost five years. He'll probably spend the rest of his life like that.

What the hell happened? Three kids shared one joint. Two survived, one was destroyed for life. Was it something Anthony ate that day? Did it have anything to do with his body temperature? Was it the mood he was in when he lit that joint? Nobody knows. Not the physicians or the neurologists or the psychiatrists. All they know is that last marijuana joint destroyed this young man.

Do you understand what I'm telling you? My nephew wasn't drinking booze or wine or beer when he smoked that reefer. He wasn't popping pills or dropping acid. He lit up a joint, like he did hundreds, maybe thousands, of times before. This joint was different though . . .This was the one that had his name on it.

Marijuana. The innocent drug. The fun drug.

I thought that maybe the joint that put my nephew away had been treated with some kind of poison that he hadn't bargained for. One of his buddies had saved the roach. I took it and had it analyzed at the police lab. It was clean. The kids hadn't been gypped.

Dope smokers worry about getting gypped. What concerns them most is buying pot that had been cut with some benign substance, something like oregano. They don't want the potency weakened.

Of course what a pot smoker should be worrying about is that the marijuana in their possession isn't laced with something that will sure as hell blow them away. Something like PCP. Angel dust.

Angle dust is a powerful hallucinogen that's derived from a tranquilizer that's used on horses. It will blow your mind. Don't let anyone tell you different. What is especially sad is the fact that most of the kids who suffer irreparable brain damage from it, didn't even know that they were using it. The marijuana that they bought was laced with the poison, but they weren't told.

I'll tell you something that will make you sick. Kids are telling me every day that there are people all over this country who are stuffing the joints that they are using and selling with their own concoction that they call dust. I know of at least 50 "recipes" they use and they are all deadly. Here's one. They grind up some dried parsley leaves, then they add rat poison. They spread out the mixture and sprinkle it with roach powder. Some of them spice it up with a little Drano or Clorox.

They don't give a damn how they get high so long as they get it.

Then they mix this shit through the marijuana and roll it into a joint, and they smoke it and sell it to the kids.

Why? Because they are building a tolerance to the drug that they are using and they need a boost. They don't give a damn how they get high so long as they get it.

School children are smoking this poison. They are taking it into their lungs and it's carried to their brain. It's no secret. I'm not the only person who knows this is going on. Have you heard about it? Has it been on the news in your town? Doesn't anyone give a damn?

I recently visited a mental institution where six teen-agers — all victims of angel dust—were in custody. They were completely crazy, unmanageable. The doctors didn't know what to do with them so they were locked up in padded rooms, wearing plastic helmets that they couldn't take off. The chin straps were locked in place. Do you know why? Because these kids, all of them, repeatedly banged their heads against the wall. I don't know why. I got the impression no one knows why. But whatever it was that was happening in their brains was unbearable.

Did the parents of these kids believe that an occasional joint was the same as an occasional highball?

A while back I visited a jail in New York. I walked through the cell block with a cop I've known for years. A kid in one of the cells called to me.

"Mister, I gotta talk to you. I need help, please talk to me."

"What's the problem, son?" I asked. "What can I do for you?"

He lowered his voice so my friend couldn't hear.

"I've been here seven days already, and they won't let me call my father. Please, I'll give you the number. Call my father. Tell him I'm in trouble. I need him."

He was in trouble all right, but his father would never be able to help him.

The cop told me the story. This boy was a nice kid, never been in trouble before. College student, upper middle class. He smoked marijuana, but wasn't considered a heavy smoker. A couple of months ago he was hit with angel dust. Someone had stuffed a joint that he smoked with it.

After the party, he walked into the house where he lived with his family. Took a gun out of his father's desk drawer, went into his parents' bedroom and killed them both. Then he killed his little sister.

He doesn't know they're dead. He doesn't remember killing them. He had been in jail two months and every day he cries for his father to come and help him.

Did someone tell him that marijuana was no more dangerous than tobacco? The joint that had his name on it.

Is this an isolated case? No! These cases are happening across the country and you would be shocked if you knew how many times kids tell me they are thinking of killing their parents!

Not long ago an 18 year old boy was picked up in Baltimore. When the cops spotted him, he was running down the street. Screaming, stark naked. They caught him, wrapped him in a blanket, and got him to the police station where they tossed him into a cell.

I wasn't there, but the sergeant who was on duty told me what happened. The kid was letting out bloodcurdling screams and the other prisoners were yelling for him to shut up. Finally the sergeant went back to quiet him. The noise was driving everyone up the wall.

He approached the kid's cell, then stopped dead in his tracks. His knees began to buckle and he was hit by a wave of nausea.

The kid's face was pressed between the bars. His arms stretched out into the walkway. Blood covered his face and dripped from his fingers. With his own hands, he had clawed his eyes out.

Why did he smoke that joint?

The one with his name on it. Why?

Everywhere I go kids come up to me and want reassurance.

"Mr. Toma," they say, "Some people can handle drugs better than others, right? I mean, without getting hurt. I been smoking pot for three or four years and so far nothing's happened to me. Maybe I got a stronger system, maybe I'm just lucky, right?"

I had one of these kids the other day. He was in his junior year of high school. He was dishevelled, sloppily dressed. He looked as if he had slept in his jeans and tee-shirt.

We met outside the school building. It was a nice day but not very bright.

"Why are you wearing sunglasses?" I asked him.

I asked him a few questions about his family, school, his plans.

His father was a CPA, his mother went back to college working on a masters. He didn't get along with either of them, and he was splitting the minute he graduated from school.

What about school? He was putting in time. That's all he had to do to pass. School bored him. Didn't keep his interest. He couldn't concentrate on the crap they taught.

"What can you concentrate on?" I asked him. "Do you read? Play chess? Follow the news?"

"I listen to a lot of rock. Got friends. We just hang around."

There aren't any lucky pot smokers. Not unless they quit, before the damage is irreversible.

This kid may be only a couple of joints away from being the kind of horror story that makes you want to throw up.

When it comes to mental health care, this nation is not in good hands.

When it comes to mental illness that was caused by marijuana, almost all of the professionals are inept at best, and in many cases, an absolute danger to their patients. Not many of them have done their homework where pot is concerned. Or if they have, they reject the research. Or they smoke pot themselves. Or they just don't give a damn. Whatever the reason, a patient has to search hard and long to find someone in the mental health field who knows what the hell is going on.

There have to be some who care, but I haven't run into many. Dr. Harold Voth of the Menninger Foundation in Topeka, Kansas and Dr. Albert Honig of the Delaware Valley Mental Health Foundation in Doylestown, Pa. are two who know what's happening. Dr. Voth, in his pamphlet, "How to get your Child Off Marijuana" talks about doctors, especially psychiatrists who still claim that marijuana is harmless.

"The simple truth is that even in the mental health fields there are some people who are emotionally disturbed and have weak personalities. They tend to support far-out lifestyles and are often hostile toward authority. It is difficult for these people to take a firm stand on the side of an issue which demands excellence, maturity, etc. . . ."

So I'm telling you now, get off drugs when you can still make that decision for yourself.

Because the chances of you finding someone who can help you when your condition becomes desperate are very slim.

I met a young clinical psychologist recently. You'll run into thousands like him before you stumble across a Honig or a Voth. He was a good young man who really cares about the kids he works with. It only took a few minutes into the conversation to see that this man was truly sincere about his work, deeply moved by the pain suffered by his patient, and totally useless to anyone who came to him with a pot-induced mental illness. He smoked pot.

"Marijuana is not a problem," he said. "Anyone who is stable, who has his head on straight can handle it."

He doesn't know! This man tries to help kids every day who smoke pot — their parents pay him to help — and he doesn't know what marijuana does to his patients.

He tossed a lot of goodies at me, like, "Sure a lot of sick people smoke pot and they end up in mental hospitals and prisons. But what about all the sick people who don't smoke pot who end up in mental hospitals and prisons?"

What in the hell kind of argument is that? A lot of people don't die of cancer, so does that mean that we don't have to worry about cancer?

There's more. "What in the hell isn't harmful to us in this day and age? The air we breathe, the water we drink. Our food is contaminated with additives. Noise, stress. Everything is supposed to be bad for us. Pot's just one of a long list of things you are supposed to worry about. Where do you draw the line?"

I thought of all of the kids I've met, with pink eyes and that fogged-up look. Kids who have come up to me and said, "Mr. Toma, I'm scared. I get so confused that I can't remember what class I'm supposed to go to. I can't follow a conversation, I can't read, I can't study, I'm numb." God forbid that any of them find their way into that psychologist's office.

"Most of my friends in school smoked marijuana. Those I'm still in touch with are doing all right. And I'm doing all right."

He's not doing all right! His attitude has to be hurting the kids he is supposed to be helping. He seemed incapable of accepting the fact that marijuana is as dangerous as any drug sold on the street. He was passionate about his position. I was attacking his "friend." Marijuana makes him feel good, and he didn't like to hear me say bad things about it. He wasn't interested in knowing about THC, he was only interested in warding off the attack.

What does this psychologist tell the parents of a pot-smoking kid who come to him because they're worried about their child? You can lay odds that he puts their mind at rest. "Don't worry, Mom and Dad, pot's no worse than the cigarette you're smoking or the glass of wine you have with your dinner." He should have his license taken away from him. He's a danger to our children!

He's not doing all right, and neither are his friends if they are still blowing pot. They are all in their middle thirties, and they don't know what damage is taking place inside of them. They don't know until they smoke their next joint if it's the one that might blow their minds.

It's hard to blame this young man for being what he is.

I agreed with the young psychologist that kids have to be given the freedom to make decisions. They must learn from their mistakes and be responsible for their actions. But he's full of crap when he suggests that kids should decide whether or not they will use drugs. You wouldn't sit by and watch a kid eat rat poison so he could learn from the experience, you wouldn't sit by and watch him jump off the roof of your house with a paper kite. And it's just as idiotic if you knowingly allow a kid to smoke grass without intervening.

My wife just handed me a newspaper clipping. An Ann Landers' column. It included a letter from a 13 year old girl. Her mother is a well known psychologist in Vermont, the child said. The girl told her mother that she had recently started to smoke pot. She wanted her mother to stop her, she said, but her mother let her down. This professional shrink told her 13 year old daughter that she was old enough to make her own decisions! Well, the girl hadn't quit yet. Is this woman crazy? Would her response have been the same if her daughter had said, "Mother, I'm shooting up heroin. Should I quit?" Would her response have been the same if the girl said, "Mother, I'm thinking about committing suicide. What do you think?" What kind of a mother is she? What kind of a shrink? The next joint that child smokes might blow her away. So what would she have learned from her exercise in decision making.

There are some decisions that a child can't afford to make.

I hope this particular girl listened to the advice of Ann Landers, who is a hell of a lot smarter than a lot of the psychologists that I've met.

If you are a parent seeking help for a child, shop around before seeing a psychologist or a psychiatrist. Find out, up front, what the doctor's attitude is about marijuana and other street drugs. If he tells you that pot smoking — even in moderation — is nothing to worry about, hang up the phone. He's not for you.

The father of a 15 year old girl who has been seeing a psychologist on the advice of her school counselor told me this story. He caught her stealing money out of his wallet. She had gotten away with it for several months. First, a dollar or two. Then, five or ten. The time before she got caught she made off with $40. What did she need the money for? Marijuana and vodka.

This girl is typical of millions of kids. She was a good student until she started smoking pot. Now she was failing. She hated her parents and her teachers. She did nothing productive. Didn't babysit (thank God), wouldn't take a summer job. She'd been sexually active since she was 12—that's when she began fooling around with dope.

The psychologist, a young woman, called for a family conference after seeing the girl once a week for two months. She met with the three of them, then had a short private session with the parents.

The parents told the shrink everything that they could think of. How their daughter's personality had changed dramatically. How she cuts school, steals, uses filthy language in front of them, how they can't control her, on and on. The father had read some things about marijuana that frightened him.

"Mustn't we get her off of that drug before anything else?" he asked.

"Marijuana is just one symptom of your daughter's problem. Once we get to the root of her problems, once she understands them and is willing to face them and once she learns how to cope with these problems, then marijuana will not be a problem either."

The father was right. The psychologist was dead wrong. Psychotherapy is useless to a chronic marijuana smoker. Nothing can help until the kid stops smoking pot. The user must quit to be helped. And quitting doesn't mean laying off for a few days. They must stay off until the THC has left the brain and the body. That may take three months. The only way a psychiatrist, a psychologist, a family doctor, or a parent can help is to do everything possible to keep that user away from drugs and alcohol. Psychoanalysis for these kids is a waste of money and uses up valuable time. Psycho-active medication and drug-substitutes can be the worse thing that can be done.

I'm not saying that drug addicts (anyone who can't or won't quit using drugs) do not have problems that ordinarily might be helped by counselling. What I am saying is that a THC infected brain can not deal with the counselling.

Psychiatrists who think that Freud has any answers for them are mistaken. There was no marijuana, as potent as we know it today, when Freud was practicing his profession and writing about it.

I don't know what it is going to take to get the mental health care professionals on the right track. Those who

do not realize that this country is in the midst of a mental breakdown, and that marijuana may be the major cause, must be paralyzed from the neck up and should surrender their licenses.

I never did any research in a laboratory. I never pumped marijuana smoke into the lungs of a rat or dropped acid on a rabbit, but I think that I have listened to more kids who use drugs than anyone else in the world.

I never did any research in a laboratory. I never pumped marijuana smoke into the lungs of a rat or dropped acid on a rabbit, but I think that I have listened to more kids who use drugs than anyone else in the world.

Here is one story that I have followed for a long time. It demonstrates how dangerous it is when a kid can't trust his parents or his teachers or his doctors to know what marijuana is all about.

Danny was a terrific kid. He grew up in a happy home. His parents were college educated, interested in the world around them, and actively involved in their community. They weren't just a family, they were friends.

Danny was a successful kid, a top student, good athlete and editor of his school's paper. He was popular with boys and girls alike, and twice was elected president of the student council. His parents, grandparents, aunts and uncles—everybody— were proud of him. He always had a "steady" girl. A different one almost every semester. Danny was not a kid who was deprived of love and attention. He wanted to become a psychiatrist; his counselor at school thought that he should go into law or politics.

When he started his senior year his favorite teacher invited him and a half dozen other kids to his apartment for a rap session.

They talked politics, art, and philosophy. After the first meeting they decided to make this a regular weekly affair.

Mr. Burgess didn't want to open this up to the whole senior class, so they all agreed to keep the sessions as quiet as they could—he didn't want to be forced into turning this into a "school activity." The kids were flattered. Mr. Burgess became Bo. They had become part of an elite group in their all-white, very conservative, suburban school.

One evening, at Bo's apartment, the conversation got around to the works of Aldous Huxley. The teacher brought out the book Doors to Perception. In this book Huxley deals with his experiment with drugs and what happened when he wrote under their influence. I think Huxley used LSD, something Bo Burgess warned the kids against. But before the evening was over, he brought out a couple of joints, and Danny and the others had their first experience with marijuana.

The teacher didn't think that he was going to hurt anyone. He didn't dream that what he was beginning would turn into a nightmare for more than one of his favorite students. He loved these kids, and they trusted him.

Pot was fun. Their conversations seemed more meaningful, more arty. They all began writing poetry and songs. Danny's stuff excited everyone—his poetry was full of weird imagery, mystical abstractions. Everyone agreed that he should become a writer.

The group was made up of four girls and three boys. Four males including the teacher. And before long sex became part of the weekly activity.

One of the girls couldn't handle the pot and the sex. She became very depressed, her behavior erratic. Her parents became worried, began to probe, and the girl told all.

A couple of weeks before graduation, Mr. Burgess resigned from his teaching position.

Danny's mother was furious when the scandal broke. She was outraged by the teacher's behavior. He should have been thrown in jail, she thought. Danny's father had a different attitude. The girls were old enough to be responsible for what they did. The teacher was a young man and only human. It sure as hell didn't bother him that his son was sexually active, although he would have killed any man who tried to get his daughter in bed.

The fact that Bo Burgess introduced his kid to pot didn't really bother him at all. The only thing that worried him was the fact that marijuana was illegal. As far as he was concerned pot was no more harmful than beer. So long as it was used in moderation, he thought, there could be no problem.

"One or two joints a week or one or two cocktails—what's the difference?" he argued with his wife.

You can't blame him, he didn't know. Everybody was saying the same thing.

Danny graduated from high school with no problems, although for the first time in his public school career he didn't make with honors. Then he was off to college. He enrolled in a state university about thirty-five miles from his town; and took an apartment near the campus with a couple of his friends. He continued to smoke pot on weekends, but did okay in his freshman year.

As a sophomore he began to run into problems. He couldn't keep his mind on his books. Began missing classes, spending more time in his room listening to records, and writing poetry. His writing became more and more abstract, more mystical-fantasy, less structure. It got to the point where what he wrote made no sense to anyone but himself.

Soon he dropped out of school.

His two roommates moved out of the apartment and a girlfriend moved in. She wasn't a student, but worked on campus. She drank a little but stayed free of drugs.

The girl cared about him, and convinced him that he needed help. He made an appointment with a psychologist.

That boy should have been on the road to recovery. He admitted that he had a problem! He went for help! Do you know how important that is? But he made a mistake. He went to a clinical psychologist who didn't know that marijuana affected the brain. I'm not dumping on psychologists, it wouldn't have made a difference if he had gone to a psychiatrist, or an internist or a podiatrist. None of them knew anything about pot-related mental problems.

His mother begged him to quit smoking marijuana. She never went to medical school, but she begged him to quit. He should have listened to her, instead of listening to the shrink. That's right, my friends, because the clinical psychologist who was charging him a dollar a minute told him that a couple of joints a week couldn't hurt him. He was suffering from anxieties, the shrink told him, because he wasn't able to get in touch with his hostility. Then an MD colleague prescribed a tranquilizer for Danny

The combination of pills and pot had to make matters worse and they did. His behavior was bizarre. He would throw a temper tantrum, then slip into a deep depression. He increased the number of joints he was smoking to where he was getting high every day. His shrink increased the number of pills he was to take. Danny became paranoid and began hallucinating. At first he thought that he was developing super-human powers of perception. ESP. But soon he became suspicious and frightened of everybody and everything around him.

His girlfriend couldn't handle him anymore, but before she

moved out of the apartment she called Danny's parents.

"He's real sick," she told Danny's mother. "You better get him in a hospital."

While his mother called the family doctor for advice, his father drove to Danny's apartment. The door was locked and Danny didn't answer. The man climbed the fire escape and crawled through a small window. At first he thought Danny was gone, but the apartment door was bolted on the inside. Then he heard a noise that sounded like the whimpering of a wounded animal. It came from behind a closed door.

Danny was huddled in the corner of the small cluttered space. He was covered with a blanket, and he was shivering. His teeth chattering.

At first the boy didn't recognize his father's voice. When he felt the man's hand on his shoulder he begged.

"Please, don't kill me. I didn't do anything. I'm not a spy."

The family doctor recommended a psychiatrist who arranged for Danny to go to a mental hospital. It is one of those fancy private places that looks like a country club. Rolling hills beautifully landscaped. Handsome cottages to house the patients for $1,000 per week (they're higher now). No wonder Danny's parents felt relieved when he signed himself into the facility. He couldn't hurt himself here, they thought. At least here we would be safe.

Bullshit! That boy wasn't safe. There wasn't a doctor on that hospital staff that knew a thing about marijuana-related mental illness.

One of the saddest things about this story is that Danny may have been on his way to recovery before he entered the hospital.

You see, there was a two week wait before the hospital had a bed for Danny. His father took off work and between him and the mother they never left Danny's side. The father slept on the floor next to his bed. By the time Danny was admitted to the hospital, he was no longer hallucinating. He was suffering from intense anxiety but his paranoia had subsided. He hadn't smoked a joint for those two weeks. The doctor who arranged for his hospitalization felt that a four or five week stay in a protective institution would do wonders for the boy. Man, was he ever wrong.

The first thing they did was put him on a regimen of powerful anti-psychotic tranquilizers. He was a heavy pot smoker, and although he hadn't touched the stuff for two weeks, he came into that hospital with his brain full of THC—he didn't need more chemicals in his head. He needed time to get rid of the garbage that was already in there. Within a week he was hallucinating again. His paranoia had returned and he was diagnosed as suffering from schizophrenic-paranoia.

He sure as hell was no problem for the staff. He was spaced-out on the drug and was docile and lethargic. He didn't get out of that hospital in four to six weeks as the admitting doctor anticipated. After a year, a new psychiatrist was assigned to him. This guy slugged him with a daily dose of 160 milligrams of a drug that was rarely given in doses that exceeded 20 milligram—more than six times the maximum recommended by its manufacturer. They kept pumping this quantity into him daily for nine months.

Danny's parents were worried, their son was throwing up every day, his hair began to fall out, he had trouble keeping his eyes in focus. His father sent away for all the literature that he could find about the drug, and what he received terrified him. The drug—at the quantities they were giving him—could destroy their son.

Danny's father rushed to the hospital and confronted the doctor with the material. The doctor was obviously irritated at the father's intrusion, but laughed at his concern. Danny was in the hands of the professionals. Besides, they were planning to reduce the dosage anyway. But it was too late.

The next day a tremor in his limbs developed, and they cold-turkeyed him off the drug. Were they crazy? After almost two years of heavy daily doses of psychotropic drugs they cut it off completely.

Danny went wild, he was in agony—he was climbing the walls.

This mental hospital, like most mental hospitals, was not set up to cure sick patients. They were custodial. Now that they couldn't keep him drugged, they didn't know what to do with him. So they locked him up in a padded room.

Do you know how long these fancy doctors in their fancy hospital kept this boy caged up. Three months!

The records show that there was no therapy. Doctor's visits lasted three or four minutes! There was no diversion for the boy. No books, no radio, no paper or pencil. Everything stopped except the bills. $1,000 per month.

Danny went mad during those months. He lost his ability to communicate. He spoke in gibberish that was incomprehensible.

Finally his parents were called in.

"We've done all that we can for your son," they were told, "we suggest that you commit him to a state institution. We need the space."

Such doctors are worse than criminals on the street. They have a license to destroy life. They don't honor the trust that's given them.

Like pompous asses they take our money and convince us that they know what they are doing. They pretend that they give a damn. They give a damn all right—about being recipients of large grants, but not about the lives that are entrusted to them.

If you are a kid and you are smoking dope, you better stop now. You don't know how much THC your brain can absorb, and once it blows your mind you are going to have a hell of a time finding a professional who knows enough about marijuana to help you.

Danny's parents didn't follow the advice of the doctors. They didn't commit their son to a state institution where he would have been a custodial case for the rest of his life. After a frantic search they found a small hospital that believed that Danny could not be cured or helped with any psychotropic drugs. They worked at decoding his gibberish, and after 3½ years Danny is coming back.

With love, not drugs—with sensitive caring, not electric shock—with touching, not a padded cell, Danny is coming back.

It has taken a long time to undo the abuse of the first hospital, but it looks like in another few months Danny will be able to leave the hospital and pick up the pieces of his life that was almost shattered. Shattered by marijuana and professionals who do not know enough about the drug, or care enough about their patients.

If the physicians don't know the truth about marijuana and shrinks don't know, if the politicians don't know, and the educators don't know, then how in the hell can the children find out?

The parents owe it to their children to find out the truth. And the parents better love their children and learn to communicate with them, so when they do have the information, their kids will listen.

Right now the kids are listening to their friends, and the dope peddlers, and celebrities who get on television talk shows and news programs and spout off on subjects they know nothing about.

When you're on television people listen. Too often the wrong people have the cameras turned on them and the damage they do can be devastating when they don't know what they are talking about. When Paul McCartney, one of the most beloved rock stars in history, got arrested in Tokyo last January with eight ounces of marijuana in his bags, it was big news. Every newspaper and newscast carried the story, and Paul suddenly became an authority on the dangers of marijuana. On ABC's 20/20 show he told millions of viewers that he would continue to smoke marijuana because grass was less damaging than Scotch or tobacco. He just doesn't know what he's talking about! The point is, because the former Beatle is a superstar he can get on national television and say anything he wants to, no matter how wrong it is. His appearance on 20/20 was a free commercial for the dope pushers. The networks ought to be ashamed of themselves.

I love Hugh Downs, he does a lot of good work. I wanted to rebut Paul McCartney's comments, but he didn't. Like so many other responsible media people he has swallowed the line about marijuana being safe!

TV and radio do a real number on all of us. They don't worry about the damage they do, their eyes are glued on the local and national ratings. They extol drugs directly and by inference.

How many of you saw the special edition of 60 Minutes, the night of the National Election? In one segment Mike Wallace interviewed a young woman, the daughter of a leading politician. For some reason that I'll never understand, he needed her opinions on premarital sex and drugs.

She tried to be candid. "I don't believe in sex without love," was her answer to the premarital sex question. Terrific! What does that mean to a 13-year old girl who has a crush on a 15-year old boy? Premarital sex is okay, right? How many times will a 13 year old fall in love before she grows into a woman and finally marries? Isn't 60 Minutes saying it's all right to climb in bed with a boy just as long as you're "in love"? The girl got no argument from Mike Wallace, he wasn't concerned with the impact such a statement might have on prime time television. Next question.

Wallace thought that America needed to know this girl's opinion of drugs. Why? If he wanted someone's thoughts on drugs, why didn't he invite someone like Dr. Harold Voth of Menninger's Foundation on the show—or me?

The girl seemed a little puzzled by the question. There was a pause, then Wallace modified the question a little. It was "hard" drugs he was asking about, not marijuana! Then he muttered something that tossed pot aside as though it was inconsequential, an accepted fact of American life.

I wanted to push my fist through the TV set. I felt sick to my stomach. Millions of kids want to be told that the grass they smoke is safe. They worry about it, and God knows, they should. Too many of our media stars are sending out the wrong message to them.

Mike Wallace is no authority on marijuana. He obviously doesn't know if pot is less damaging than heroin or cocaine or acid. And Paul McCartney sure as hell doesn't know what he's talking about—he's a user. He has no idea what the THC and hundreds of other poisonous chemicals in marijuana are doing to his body right now—or what is going on in the fatty tissues of his brain. If he did he'd probably warn the world about it in no uncertain terms!

No one has a right to proclaim to millions of adoring fans that marijuana is okay—I think that it should be a crime to lead kids down a path that for them might end up in a mental institution, a prison, or a morgue.

Why should the networks allow entertainers to contaminate the airways with such dangerous misinformation?

It seems to me that it's a lot easier to get a pro-drug message on the air, than an anti-drug message. Did you ever listen to the records and tapes that are being sold to our kids, and played by plenty of radio disc jockeys? Some of the lyrics are sick. Lots of them are slightly coded so the parents who are paying for the albums won't know what the hell they are buying. Like, "Lucy in the Sky with Diamonds." Lucy = L/Sky = S/Diamonds = D. LSD. Cute, huh? There are about 400 drug records listed in the Rock Music Source Book. Titles like Purple Haze, Candy Man, White Rabbit, The Acid Queen, Mayrowanna, Take a Whiff, Legalize It, Mary Jane. Man, it's sick.

Here's something that will blow your mind. In New York City and probably in other major cities there are cable TV stations that regularly report street-drug activity—for the users! Like a shopper's guide. The night I saw it, the commentator—a young single mother—reported that a big pot bust had caused the price of Colombian marijuana to go sky high. But she had good news — there was plenty of hashish around and the price was down. She urged the pot smokers who had never tried hash before to try it now. "You'll get a great high," she promised our kids.

What in the hell is going on in this country? Why in the hell can people like this hide behind the First Amendment? How many potheads and coke snorters are holding down high media positions? Is this nation going crazy?

"Stop killing yourselves with that garbage!"

It absolutely kills me when people with the Proper Credentials make pro-marijuana statements. I'm talking about scientists and medical doctors. And you can bet that every time they do their words are picked up on the news wires.

The next day we read in the newspapers that pot is not so bad. People who are supposed to know better come out for decriminalization of marijuana. Do you think that kids know what that means? Ask them. Most of them will tell you that it means that it's okay to smoke it but not to sell it. That is what they think. And when people who should know better suggest legalizing marijuana, every kid who smokes the weed jumps with joy. It gives them ammunition when they are confronting a non-user. And every parent who knows that his child is a user, breathes a little easier.

We sit back and let these "experts" run off their mouths without challenging them.

But why do they do it and why do we allow it? There has never been a scientific study that concludes that marijuana is a safe drug. Not a single one. And there never will be.

On the other hand, there have been hundreds of studies that show that marijuana is harmful. And there are tens of thousands of victims to support those studies. Anyone in his right mind, who is paying attention, has to be convinced.

Today a few of the experts are saying, "Oops, we made a mistake. Sorry about that." But they are not saying it loudly enough.

When a few rats were OD'd on cyclamates, the noise the experts made rated the headlines. Did you see any headlines when the data on marijuana began to trickle out? I didn't see any. They should run full page notices warning us that POT IS DESTROYING OUR CHILDREN. Every television station should show scenes of kids beating their heads against padded walls in mental institutions, and pictures of twisted, deformed babies who are the victims of their parents' marijuana highs.

The experts can't undo the harm they've already done. And they will have a hell of a time trying to slow down the drug action that they helped accelerate, but they better start spreading the word. They better hurry, before we lose the minds of a whole generation. They owe us that much.

Dr. Robert DuPont is one of the experts who used to think that marijuana is "less of a hazard to health than tobacco or alcohol." Dr. DuPont is no slouch, he made his living knowing about the effects drugs have on us. When he compared pot favorably to tobacco, he was being paid by the United States Government to know about such things. In fact, Dr. DuPont was the Director of the National Institute on Drug Abuse when he made such statements. Can you believe it? The pushers and the distributors and the smugglers were jumping with glee. It seemed as if the U.S. Government was endorsing marijuana. It would be only a matter of time when we would buy pot from vending machines like Winstons, some thought. Rumors began to fly that the major tobacco companies were gearing up to package and distribute pot.

Well, Dr. DuPont was wrong about marijuana and he has had the courage and honesty to admit it. In July of 1978 he was quoted in the Washington Post.

"I get a very sick feeling in the pit of my stomach when I hear talk about marijuana being safe. Marijuana is a very powerful agent which is affecting the body in many ways. What the full range of these consequences is going to prove to be, we can only guess at this point. But from what we already know, I have no doubt that they are going to be horrendous."

You don't have to guess about the consequences, Dr. DuPont. Visit a few mental institutions, and jails and morgues. You'll see the consequences. Travel with me to a few schools and listen to the kids. They'll tell you what pot is doing to their lives.

DuPont is on the right track now. Thank God. In the December 1979 issue of <u>Reader's Digest</u> he said that youngsters who are smoking pot are "making guinea pigs of themselves in a tragic national experiment".

"This is a disaster," he told Edwin Newman on NBC, "and I feel very badly to have contributed to that."

In April 1981, in an interview for <u>Listen,</u> Dr. DuPont told Frances Soper " . . . this threat has to do not only with lungs, with reproduction, with clearness of mind, with work efficiency, but with the quality of life itself."

This man did a 180 degree turn, and it was a brave moral thing for him to do. We need Dr. DuPont and anybody else who has the guts to fight this incredible sickness.

Dr. DuPont caught up with the research 4 years ago, and I'm sure that he's been staying on top of it ever since. But too many experts avoid the research as though it didn't exist. I heard a couple of them on national radio recently.

I was all wound up after a late session with about 4000 high school students and parents. Every meeting is exciting for me, but I was especially high this night because the parents were exceptionally open and demonstrative. Some kids were hugged and kissed by their parents for the first time in years. They weren't ashamed to cry as they reached out to one another. It was good.

Anyways, I couldn't sleep and sometime after 2 AM I turned on the radio. A national telephone call-in show was on the air. The president of a state lung association and a psychologist and president of an American lung association were the guests of Larry King.

I knew that they couldn't talk about lung disorders without discussing the damage marijuana inflicts. Terrific. The public needs this kind of information. And here on national radio were two experts who head prestigious organizations to pass on some vital information. Did they do it? No way. When the phone calls came in asking about pot, they didn't know their ass from their elbow.

The first caller I heard was a young man who wanted to know if marijuana was more harmful to the lungs than tobacco. The experts told him, and the rest of the listeners, that tobacco smoke had more cancer producing carcinogens than marijuana smoke. They are wrong. Absolutely, positively, dead wrong. I couldn't believe it.

Later, a woman from Florida called to take issue with their answer. She had read that marijuana contained more than 10 times more tar and nicotine than tobacco. This woman knew more than the lung association experts. They hemmed and hawed a little but avoided responding to her.

A young male caller asked, "If marijuana is safer than tobacco so far as the lungs are concerned, just what's so terrible about it?" The answer was a disaster. The experts weren't recommending that anyone smoke pot. There wasn't enough information yet. It may take 30 years before all the data is in and the findings conclusive! These people have no business talking about marijuana on national radio or anywhere else. They don't know what they are talking about. They are damaging kids. They are undermining the work of people who know what these guys are supposed to know.

You better believe this. The pot you are smoking today is 20 times more harmful to the lungs than tobacco. 20 times! That's not my number.

The American Lung Association has that information. They know pot has more carcinogenic hydrocarbons, tar, and nicotine than tobacco. They know that the paper pot smokers prefer produces many more pollutants for the lung to deal with than the paper used for regular cigarettes.

I called the Ohio Lung Association today. The young woman who spoke with me had a pamphlet in front of her. It said in no uncertain terms that marijuana was more harmful to the lungs than tobacco. Do you know who distributed the pamphlet? The American Lung Association! Why in the hell didn't two experts know it? They are big wheels in that organization.

They ought to take this kind of expert, wrap them up in their doctoral gowns and drop them in the middle of the Atlantic Ocean. We don't need this kind of expert. We need people who care enough to do their homework. People who give a damn.

We need our government too. But so far they have done us more harm than good in dealing with the drug problem.

Do you know that we're the only country in the world that hasn't taken a really hard stand against marijuana?

Do you know that we're the only nation in the whole world that has considered legalizing marijuana. And that is in spite of the fact that we are bound by international treaties not to legalize it!

Does our government know something good about marijuana that no one else in the world knows? Is that why they have allowed this nation to become the number one market place for the world's pot growers? Is that why our children have become the illegal traffickers' best customers? Do you think that maybe our government has discovered that marijuana contains a new vitamin that cures acne? No way. Pot is a killer.

So why are the officials sitting on their hands? Maybe it's because we've elected so many corrupt, perverted, immoral, alcoholic politicians into office that we have no one to protect us.

Why in the hell are so many of them pressing for decriminalization of marijuana? It's exactly what organized crime wants! It takes the pressure off of their customers. It's like the government is giving its stamp of approval to marujuana use. The eleven states that have already decriminalized pot is saying to its people, "Destroy yourself with 421 different chemicals, we don't give a damn about you, but you little guys better stay out of the business!" You know damned well that Organized Crime doesn't give a crap about the law. They're not worried about the government interfering with their business, but they don't like competition. Decriminalization is a joke—a sick joke—and the joke's on us!

I've been in every one of the states that has gone soft on pot and I can tell you that the drug epidemic is worse than ever. It looked like my state, New Jersey, was going to be the 12th state that went that route. Many of our high officials were pushing for it, but thank God that Chris Jackson was a tough Speaker of the House. He knew better, and he had the guts to fight it. He had me address the full assembly and the next day the wire services credited me with shooting down the decriminalization bill. Chris Jackson deserves the credit. Every state needs people as tough and honest as he is, in high places.

What is the Justice Department's Drug Enforcement Administration doing for us? Dammit, they are employed by us. Our taxes pay their salaries. The problem is that too many of these public servants are on two payrolls. We pay them and the criminals pay them. Peter Bensinger who heads the DEA admits it. He said some DEA agents and other law enforcement officials are being bought off by organized crime and "private entrepreneurs".

In a recent column by Carl T. Rowan, Bensinger complains that his administration is weakened by corruption, fear, soft judges, crippling federal laws and, of course, inadequate manpower. But more manpower is not the answer because there are so many ways to bring drugs into this country, and the stakes are so high that there's always an army of people willing to take the chance. The answer is in the home. Remember, if there's no demand there's no supply.

It's important that we don't allow ourselves to be depressed when we hear the truth. Feeling sorry for ourselves is a luxury we can't afford.

Be angry!

Feel outrage at the double-dealing traitors who serve two governments. The United States and its most dangerous enemy — the Government of Organized Crime.

Be angry!

Feel outrage at the smugglers who sneak in poison from foreign lands and dump it on our streets and in our schools.

Be so angry that the next time a pusher tries to sell you some dope you can scream at him, "Get the hell out of my life!"

PART 3

THE DRUG EPIDEMIC

A lot of this book is about marijuana, and for good reason. It's the most misunderstood of all the street drugs and the most unpredictable.

It permanently damages more kids and adults than any other. But don't get the idea that I take any drug lightly. I don't, and neither should you. The others are killers too. Especially alcohol. More kids drink liquor today than ever before and lots of them are alcoholics. In every batch of mail I get, there are letters from kids who tell me that they can't get through the day without booze. I'm talking about children, some of them who aren't even teenagers yet. It's hard for me to understand how kids can become alcoholics right under the noses of their parents. Adults may know nothing about street drugs, but everyone knows about booze. Most pot smokers drink. And alcohol is the #1 kid-killer in the United States. You adults remember — more people are killed by drunken drivers than by most diseases. These are the same people who yesterday said it could never happen to me. So if you think that alcohol is a safer way to get high than pot, you're wrong. The only safe way to get high is on life.

There's a myth about marijuana that has to be shot down. It's been said so often that marijuana doesn't lead to other drugs that most people believe it. Well let me tell you here and now that anyone who tells you that doesn't know what he's talking about. I've rarely met a kid who uses speed, LSD, heroin, dust, cocaine, mushrooms, or any drug that gives them a high, who didn't start off with marijuana. Pot introduces them to the feeling, and for many kids the feeling of being high becomes so damned important that they are willing to try almost anything to get it. The more pot they smoke, the more they need to get a good high. They build up a tolerance to the THC and the high that they get and try all kinds of things to boost it. So when they are offered some other drug that promises a good high they're more than willing to experiment. Getting high, that's what is important to them, and they don't care what they have to put into their bodies to get it.

The glamour drug, today, is cocaine. It costs more than $2000 an ounce and it's the craze among millions of kids and adults who are looking for a classy way to screw themselves up. $2000 an ounce for garbage! I don't know what in the hell is the matter with so many Americans. Why are they so dissatisfied with themselves that they need to put poison in their blood in order to get a thrill? They are idiots! I don't care how rich they are, how successful or famous they are— they are stupid!

Most coke is snorted and the users don't know what kind of trouble they are getting into. They're playing around with what many doctors call the "triangle of death." The points of the triangle are the two eyeteeth and the bridge of the nose. That area is more susceptible to infection than any other. Here's why. It's the only part of the body that isn't protected by the lymphatic system—and it's the lymph glands that fight off infections. Okay, so here's what happens. The coke that is taken in through the nostrils gets into the bloodstream through the mucous membranes. In doing so, it constricts the blood vessels in these membranes, reducing the blood supply, and drying up the nose. Snort enough and sores start developing, cartilage is exposed, and the septum becomes perforated. Visualize what I'm telling you — the inside of the nose and the sinus cavities become like filthy cesspools. Here is the scariest part of all. While this $2000 an ounce powder gives you the feeling that you're king of the world, for a few brief minutes before you need another hit, it can be burning a hole right through the wall of the cavity in your head.

And do you know what's on the other side of that wall? Your brain, baby, that's what's there.

And when the brain is exposed to the coke and the infections and the blisters start forming on it, you'll be screaming for help! But it might be too late. There are plastic surgeons who are making a fortune trying to patch up the holes and repair the damage. Man, you gotta be crazy to play around with your brain. I can't understand why more doctors, especially ear, nose and throat specialists, don't cry out to the world on the dangers of this cocaine epidemic. Why do they remain silent? It never ceases to amaze me how many thousands of people a day are shocked when I explain this. They should be hearing it from their doctors!

And like every other plaything that starts off as a toy for the rich and the powerful, and eventually is mass-marketed—cocaine is now as available as pot or speed. And of course the kids are getting their share. The quality is not as good, more imperfections, more chance for serious damage. But you can find it in every school, in every city and town. And when the teacher is in front of the class wondering if anything he says is getting through to the students, the kids are thinking about the shit that they have in their pockets and purses and waiting for the chance when they can get their next blast. It's sick.

There's no way in hell you teachers or parents are going to educate these kids with all these drugs flowing like water. They're not reachable in this condition. While many of you teachers are trying to do the best you can, how can you expect to reach them when many are high right in class? They admit it to me! And many kids who aren't high have their hands in their pockets feeling the drugs in their pockets thinking about how high they'll get at lunchtime or after school. You're not educating these kids, you're just going through the motions.

Most parents are shocked when they find out that their children are into drugs. The younger the kid the bigger the blow.

They can't imagine that a kid who collects Star Wars models or Nancy Drew books knows about reefers and roaches and bongs.*

The idea that their innocent little kid might be getting high three or four times a day is absolutely mind-boggling.

"How can this happen?" they want to know.

"Why," they cry. "why do they do it?"

Why in hell would a kid who hasn't yet reached puberty take that first lungful of marijuana or that first swallow of alcohol?

The two answers that I hear most often are, "I saw other kids doing it and it looked like fun," and "My friends talked me into it."

Once they tried it, they liked it. They liked the feeling the chemicals gave them. And they liked the feeling of becoming one of the crowd.

There's nothing so shocking about those reasons, is there? Ask any adult why he drinks and he will tell you the same thing. He likes the feeling and the sociability. Some adults claim that they drink because they like the taste of liquor and wine. Who are they kidding? How many of them would pay $10-12 for a fifth of vodka if it didn't contain alcohol? No one could make a living selling alcohol-free scotch.

People drink liquor, pop pills, snort coke, sniff glue, and smoke grass because they like the way it makes them feel.

*Reefers are Marijuana Cigarettes.
Roaches are the butts of these cigarettes.
Bongs are sphere-shaped pipes.

Just like their parents, kids found out that certain chemicals make them more relaxed and less inhibited. They seem smarter and funnier and more acceptable.

Okay, so kids see others doing drugs and alcohol and they want to join the fun. But not all of them simply jump in. Some have to be persuaded.

For some reason people who like to get high don't enjoy being around people who don't get high. They don't even enjoy being around people who are high on life. They want their friends to be high on chemicals.

I've gone through this a million times. I'm having dinner with someone who doesn't know me very well and the waiter wants to take an order for cocktail or wine. I ask for soda or juice and my dinner partner tries to coax me into having a highball. He doesn't want to drink alone, he says. What the hell does he think I'm planning to do with my tomato juice? Eat it with a fork? It's weird. He doesn't insist that I put pepper on my salad or gravy on my mashed potatoes, but he sure is uncomfortable if I don't put scotch in my soda.

The pressure on the kids to use dope is tremendous. They get it in the school, in the playground, at the community center, at camp, in the drive-in movies.

Drug users love to turn other kids on. The more the merrier. It makes them feel safer. They get a kick out of it, like spreading gossip or telling a dirty joke.

And of course there are the professionals who work right in the schools. The pushers whose business it is to turn on as many kids as possible. These kids are dynamite salespeople.

I talked to a fourteen year old girl today who told me that she has been selling as many as 300 joints a day in her suburban school. That's a lot of dope.

By the time a youngster gets into junior high school the pressure is unbelievable. The kids who aren't doing drugs are considered freaks. And many of them feel like freaks. They are on the outside of the school's high society looking in. Life on the "inside" looks so appealing to them. The users seem to be having all the fun. They appear cool, loose, easygoing; they don't give a damn. Like the cool cats in Mr. Kotter's class.

So the pressure is put on them. The parents are rarely any help to the kids who try to resist. Neither are the teachers. The straights are made fun of, challenged, snowed. And most of them cave in under the pressure.

Besides aggressive peer pressure, there is plenty of subtle outside pressure that takes its toll. Too many of their media idols use dope and don't keep it a secret. I mean stars like the Rolling Stones and Paul McCartney. You could fill a telephone directory with their names. Rock concerts are drug events, and nobody seems to give a damn. Hip movies like Cheech and Chong's "Up in Smoke" glorify drugs and so do TV shows like "Saturday Night Live." Everybody seems to be doing it and having fun, and the anti-drug voices are so soft and tentative that they can't be heard.

Plenty of kids try to resist the pressure at first, but most of them can't handle it.

You probably know why. They haven't developed any self-control. They haven't had enough practice saying no when it's easier and more fun to say yes.

This is the age of no "shoulds" and no "shouldn'ts". This is the age when you can do almost anything so long as you don't get caught, and it's usually no big deal even if you do get caught.

And kids don't resist drugs out of fear. Who do they fear? Their parents? Teachers? The Law? God?

And most of them don't resist out of love and respect. That's because they don't respect their parents or their teachers or the Law or God. But most of all they don't respect themselves!

Maybe these last statements should be softened a little. I suppose a child can use drugs and still love and respect his parents. That might be true if the parents he loves use drugs themselves — and demonstrate to the child that they accept mind-altering, mood-altering drugs.

And what about pills? What's scary about them? Kids learn from day one that pills can take away pain, make them feel good. Their bathroom cabinets are loaded with them, and mom probably carries a jewel studded pill box in her purse.

Got a headache? Take a pill? Coming down with something? Take a pill. Depressed? Take a pill. Hyper? Take a pill. Can't sleep? Take a pill. Can't get started in the morning? Take a pill. Too fat? Take a goddam pill.

Decide how you want to feel, what mood you want to be in—then head for the medicine cabinet or the liquor cabinet. Or if you're a kid, check out your own stash—the drugs you have hidden away.

The pressure to use mood-altering drugs is tremendous. Right?

Who is pressuring the kids not to do drugs? The truth is—almost no one!

If 100% of the parents were taking pot seriously, maybe 10% of the kids would be experimenting with it instead of the great majority of them.

But most parents know nothing about pot. Most don't know what a joint looks like. They wouldn't recognize a dime bag or a roach clip if they found one in their kids' lunch box.

Most parents still want to believe that drugs are something that happens only to blacks in the ghetto or to poor whites in the inner city, or to jazz musicians. It's like they live in a time machine that got stuck in the '50s.

Most parents are absolutely shocked when they discover that a child of theirs has slipped away from them and into the drug culture. And they can't imagine that they might have contributed to their kid's condition.

The principal of a school asked if I would talk to the parents of one of his students during the break between two of my lectures. They were terribly upset. They had recently discovered that their daughter was heavily into drugs. They couldn't reach her and wanted my advice. These people were very concerned parents. They obviously adored their child. There was nothing they wouldn't do for her. We talked about 90 minutes in a restaurant. During that time I drank two large glasses of tomato juice. The mother drank three martinis and the father three double scotches. Between them they smoked damned near a package of cigarettes! They were very upset about their daughter and nervous about discussing it with me. So they handled the stress their way—with alcohol and tobacco. How in hell could these people help that girl? They already taught her what they know about coping!

Nobody looks for trouble — especially where their children are concerned. But parents can't close their eyes and stop up their ears in order to avoid facing this problem. Parents check their kids' teeth, their eyes and their ears. They worry about their acne and their dandruff—and they should. But let me tell you something—they better make sure that the kids aren't coming down with an irreversible case of pot sickness—because you won't correct that with a pair of glasses or a hearing aid. You'll wish it were that easy.

There are parents who will never read this book because for some reason they refuse to be informed. They don't want to know what's happening. They simply refuse to consider it possible that their children might ever get involved in drugs. Even when they have damned good reason to be suspicious, they absolutely refuse to deal with it. Here is a story that demonstrates the kind of ignorance and stupidity that I'm talking about.

A lady who lived in a wealthy community near a city where I was scheduled to speak wanted to know if I could stretch my visit and talk in her daughter's junior high school. Something happened that really worried her, and she thought maybe I could help shake up her sleepy community. Her daughter belonged to a girl's club — a charitable organization that usually met in the area's community center. The parents of one of the members went away for the weekend and gave permission for the group to get together in their home. Eighteen girls attended—ages 12 to 15. A high school senior supervised the meeting. As soon as the kids finished the club business, one of the girls brought out a bag of marijuana and proceeded to roll some joints. The older girl tried to stop the kids from lighting up, but when she couldn't control them, she split. She didn't squeal on them, but she was afraid to stay.

Fifteen of the eighteen kids got stoned! The daughter of the woman who phoned me was one of the three who didn't. She told her mother what happened. And her mother reported the incident to the community center's youth activity director. The director phoned the parents of every girl who was at the meeting. He told them what happened but didn't name any of the girls who got stoned. He asked that all the parents meet at the center to discuss what he considered a frightening situation.

The meeting was held, but nobody showed up! Nobody but the woman who phoned me. The youth activity director contacted all of the parents again. What happened? Are you ready for this? Every single parent reported that they have talked to their daughters, and was happy to report that their kid was one of the three who didn't get stoned! Were all of those parents stupid? No way. Some didn't want to know. Some didn't want to get involved. Some didn't give a damn. The parents of seventeen girls had the opportunity to demonstrate to their daughters that they were concerned about them, that they cared. What was the message that they gave to their kids instead? I hear stories like this every day.

Some kids have been programmed to become addicts from the day they were born. Millions of adults are alcoholics and plenty of them have children. These kids have to be as strong as Samson to come out of their home straight.

And plenty of kids tell me that their parent do drugs. What chance do they have? An eleven year old boy told me that his mother gets high almost every evening. She blows marijuana smoke into the face of his baby sister. The little girl gets giggly and the mother thinks it's cute! She encourages the boy to take a hit on the joint. What chance does either of these kids have?

Some kids turn to dope because they can't stand the reality of their lives and they haven't developed the skills to cope with it. But that dope will prevent them from ever developing those skills!

You don't have to be smart or moral or loving or fair to become a parent. You don't even have to like children. There are plenty of rotten parents in this world and their children have to fight for their lives to survive.

Child abuse and incest are commonplace. It exists in every neighborhood in this country. A guidance counselor was recently quoted in an Ohio newspaper as saying that child beating and incest were bigger problems in his school than drugs! These kids will turn to anything to ease their pain, including drugs. Unfortunately, the drugs, like the psychotic parent, is a vicious child abuser, and in the end will destroy the children.

Most parents who read this will say, "Hold it, Toma, I'm not an alcoholic. I don't get high on drugs. I don't beat my kids.

"I love my children. I'd give them the shirt off my back. I work my ass off to provide a nice home for them, and a good life. I'll see to it that they get a college education if they want it.

"If my kids get into drugs, it's because of outside influences. Peer pressure. I can't control what's happening outside my home.

"The world has changed since I was a kid. Kids have changed. Sometimes I think we came from different planets, but I'm doing the best I can!"

It's not easy being a parent today. It's tough to raise a child in a world that seems to have gone crazy — where everything seems out of control. Right?

To students and parents at the evening session: "Your kids came to school today stoned! I'll never understand how you can let this happen!"

Well, let me tell you something my friends, it has never been easy! It wasn't easy for my parents or millions of other immigrants who came to this country penniless, uneducated and unable to speak the language. They managed though, and they didn't lose a generation of children to drugs or alcohol.

And it wasn't easy during World War II, when our country was turned upside down and families torn apart. We survived somehow, and the children didn't turn to drugs and alcohol.

So what's happening now that is causing the majority of our children to risk their lives and their futures for a chemical high? This country is not at war. There are no breadlines, and people aren't selling apples and pencils on the corners because they can't buy food.

We're not in the midst of a violent social revolution. So what's happening? Why do kids who come from decent homes with respectable parents prefer the dangerous drug culture to the straight world? What's so unattractive about their parents' world that they're rejecting it?

No parent is dumb enough to think that they play no part in shaping the attitudes and behavior of their children. Every parent demonstrates their values and their morals. Kids have a pretty good idea what their parents stand for, what they believe in. They see how their parents cope with frustrations, how they express their emotions, how they handle their relationships.

I talk to messed-up kids almost every day of my life and I meet plenty of their parents. And do you know something? Their parents, as often as not, are as screwed-up as they are.

I meet parents who are so dissatisfied with their own lives that it's impossible for them to provide a healthy home environment for their family. And I meet parents who are so egotistical, so involved with their own little worlds, that there's no room for their children in their lives. I meet workaholics whose priorities are so twisted that their jobs became their lovers and their loved ones.

Most of the messed-up parents that I meet suffer from the same thing. Lack of self-esteem. No self-respect. They have lived for 30, 40, 50 years and still don't like themselves. And they come to me every day — hurt and bewildered — and they cry, "My kids don't respect me. Why?"

I'll tell you what I tell them. If you don't respect yourself, don't expect anyone else to respect you. If you don't love yourself, don't expect love from others. Why in the hell should anyone think more of you than you think of yourself?

People who don't respect themselves are always running scared, they never feel secure. They expect to get abused and set themselves up for it. They feel guilty even when they are guiltless. These people become the dumping ground for everyone's crap, and they suffer for it. So do their loved ones. How many people, who are bullied on the job, try to build up their ego by becoming bullies at home? It's sick and it's sad.

If you want your kids to respect you, you have to demand respect from the rest of the world too. But first

you got to demand it from yourself. Set limits on the amount of abuse you will take from anyone, even if it means taking some risks. Once you make up your mind about that, you begin to feel pretty good about yourself.

I set limits and I refuse to run scared. When I was a young detective, my partner and I raided a gambling den in Newark's Spanish Harlem, the roughest section in the city. We busted about a dozen punks who were into everything—gambling, narcotics, prostitution, murder, you name it. The next day the word went out on the street that their friends were going to kill me. I got the news from a cop who got it from a stoolie. He didn't know who was going to pull the trigger or slit my throat, but there was no doubt in his mind that they were going to get me. And I'm telling you that I got scared. Scared sick. These guys were all tough mob guys and if they made up their minds to blow me away, nothing would stop them. My first reaction was to run. My family needed me alive. I'd ask for a transfer. Maybe move to another town. Maybe quit the force.

That night, after we went to bed, Patty began questioning me. I didn't tell her what was wrong, but she knew that I was in trouble. She had seen me plenty uptight before, but never like this. She was probing and I was dancing around her questions, and it suddenly struck me that unless I resolved this fear, I would never feel like a real man again. I got out of bed, told my wife that I had a job that had to be finished by morning, and took off for the Spanish ghetto.

It was after 1 AM when I got to the joint that my partner and I had raided. I had stopped on the way and dressed up like a drunken bum, stuck a gun in my belt and a toy hand grenade in my coat pocket. The place was packed when I stumbled in—more than a hundred people laughing, yelling, yakking in Spanish. No one paid any attention to me when I elbowed my way through the crowd toward a pool table that was being used for shooting craps. The noise in the room was deafening.

When I got within arm's length of the pool table, I slipped the toy grenade out of my pocket, took a deep breath and made my move. With one action I shoved aside the guy who was standing in front of me and leaped onto the table waving the toy grenade over my head and screaming like a lunatic. "THIS IS A BOMB. A BOMB!"

It wasn't long before everyone was frozen in their place and the only sound in the room was my voice.

"Do you know who I am?" I screamed, "I'm Toma. T-O-M-A. I'm the cop you bastards want to kill! Well, I'm here to make it easy for you. But when I die, everybody dies! When I fall this baby blows up!"

Nobody budged. You gotta believe that I had their attention.

"Now you better start praying every day that I die of old age, because if I get hit—no matter who does it—my friends are going to blow this place away! So you punks better start worrying about my health, you better try to keep me alive!"

When I got off the table, the crowd parted like the Red Sea to let me through. I looked into their faces as I walked toward the door. Some were frightened and surely some thought that I was crazy, but I could tell that plenty of them respected me. And I felt good about myself.

When I feel frightened or insecure, I take action to correct those crippling feelings. Maybe what I did that night was nuts, but I was willing to risk my life in order to feel like a whole person.

I see people every day who are willing to eat dirt rather than risk a confrontation. I see people every day who allow themselves to be dumped on, rather than risk a relationship or a job. You got to set limits on what you'll take from others. I don't know how you can respect yourself if you don't.

I can hear you saying "Toma, you're different. How can I apply that to my everyday life?" My friend, let me give you just one example:

A few years ago a friend of mine got a job as a salesman with a big corporation. He had a big territory, three states, and one of the first accounts he had to call on was 150 miles from his home. He drove for four and a half hours and got to the account 15 minutes early. It was a major department store. One of the clerks told him that the buyer wasn't in yet, so he opened up his sample case just to make sure that everything was in order. It was an important account, he was new and a little nervous.

Suddenly he was startled by a woman's voice, "What do you think you're doing?" she barked. It was the buyer.

He introduced himself and explained that he had a 9:30 appointment.

She pointed at a clock on the wall. "Can't you tell time? Does that say 9:30?"

He couldn't believe that she was serious. He smiled, but before he could say anything, she said in a voice that could be heard all over the department, "Don't laugh at me, buster."

A couple of customers and a clerk had stopped in their tracks and were staring at the two of them. He closed his sample case and without saying a word left the store.

That evening there was a message for him at his hotel to call his boss right away, at home. The woman had complained.

My friend explained what happened and was told to get back to her the next morning. She was expecting him. "You can't be so sensitive," his boss told him. "If you're going to keep your job and be successful you better learn to take a certain amount of crap and smile." How much crap are you supposed to take, my friend wanted to know. His boss couldn't tell him where to set the limit.

"Well, I have a rule that I set for myself. Whenever I'm in a tight situation I imagine that my ten year old son is at my side. I'll take anything that won't make my kid ashamed of me," my friend said.

His boss thought about it for a minute or two. "Will you go back if she phones you and apologizes?"

"Yep."

My friend respected himself and demanded to be treated with respect. It's paid off in many ways. Today he is National Sales Director for that company.

Here's that simple rule my friend used to resolve the problem for himself: "Whenver I'm on the receiving end of somebody's abuse, I imagine that my ten year old son is at my side. I'll take anything to the point that I think my kid would be ashamed of me. That's my limit."

Friends, if we all used that simple rule, the changes you'd see in this country would be revolutionary!

"You become a parent the day your first child is born—and you're a parent from that day on—until you die. Touch your children—tell them you love them!"

It doesn't matter what kind of work you do for a living. You can be an office worker, laborer or waitress and have dignity and self-respect.

It's your attitude and the way you feel about yourself that makes the difference. Not your title, not your income. I know plenty of executives who allow their self-esteem to be squashed by their superiors and the system under which they work. And how many rich and seemingly successful people have you heard about, who had such a low opinion of themselves that they ended their lives with a bullet or a bottle of pills? Real success has to do with the relationship you have with yourself and your loved ones.

If you are going to be happy and raise an emotionally healthy family, you have to get your values in order. You have to know what is really important in your life. You have to know where you and your wife and your kids fit into your life—and where your career and the things that you are struggling to acquire fit in. The relationship between the values you preach and the life you live has to make sense. If there's a serious conflict between the two, you are surely going to be screwed up. You can't say one thing and do another!

Fathers have to make up their minds that they must be more than just money making machines. They must realize that being a "good provider" isn't enough. The responsibility of a father is much more demanding and more important than that. The father who believes that it's the mother's job to raise the children is copping out. Children need their father's time and interest, just as they need their mother's. Things are never right for the kid who feels detached from his father's life.

Young mothers are having a tougher time now than ever before. The traditional role of the sexes is being challenged and it's confusing the hell out of a lot of us. Especially the young college-educated woman.

The Woman's Movement brought to the forefront some women, brilliant, articulate women, totally committed to one of the most important causes ever. But it also provided a vehicle for a few loud-mouth sisters, who aren't just pro-women, but also anti-man. And not pro-all-women, but pro-some-women. These fanatics weren't satisfied to bring an end to whatever injustices women face. They tried to bring about an end to the traditional family, too.

"How can you be satisfied to be just a wife, homemaker and mother?" they ask the contented woman. "You deserve more than that. You're a victim of a family structure that men invented."

"For crissake, don't settle for being just a mother. Be a dental hygienist. Don't be somebody's housekeeper. Hire a housekeeper and become somebody's plumber.

You know what's so sad about all this? They made a lot of good women wonder. They made a lot of good women question their usefulness."

"Am I really being fulfilled as a human being?" they ask themselves. "Maybe I should finish college and become a teacher."

Sweetheart, let me tell you something. If you are staying home and raising a family, you are a teacher. And a nurse. And a psychologist. You have the opportunity to be a spiritual leader, and maybe you're dealing with human life in a way that no teacher, or office manager, or lawyer deals with it. Your work is so important that it's awesome. There can be more beauty and satisfaction in your work than in any position you could ever prepare for in college.

I'll tell you something else. My wife, Patty, is a homemaker. She raised three daughters and a son, and not one of them smokes, drinks or does drugs. They are well-adjusted, happy kids who live within the law and aren't ashamed to go to church and thank God for who they are and what they have. They learned in their home that they can respect their minds and respect their bodies and be turned on by life. They learned from her that they can be popular without compromising their morals and their beliefs.

Every one of my girls looks up to her mother. They love and respect her. They know she's successful, and Patty knows it too. I'm proud of the fact that my daughters look forward to the time when they will be wives and mothers and homemakers, even though they expect to have careers. And my son won't settle for anyone who isn't sure that she wants the same thing.

A young homemaker with two children, 6 and 3 years old, told me that she was frustrated because when she looks back on a day's work she feels that she didn't accomplish very much. Most of what she did was routine, she said. She was lucky if she felt "productive" or "creative" a couple of hours a day.

Well, let that young woman visit almost any office in this country and try to find someone who's doing better. Some of the most creative people I've ever met tell me that 90% of their time is bogged down with crap-work. Paper shuffling. Doing nothing but servicing the system.

It's more difficult to be a successful mother and homemaker than it is to become a successful business person. And it's damned near impossible to be all three at the same time.

So if you're a mother, and doing a good job of it, you don't have to feel inferior to any career woman. You should be held in the highest esteem and should demand the respect you deserve.

A child needs stability in his life. He needs parents who respect themselves and each other. And he needs parents who respect him. He needs to live in a family environment that is structured. Where the parents' roles are pretty well defined, and so are his.

Kids need rules and regulations to live by, and they must know that inappropriate or irresponsible behavior is not acceptable.

The parents have to set the limits, make the rules. It's an important part of parenting and must be taken seriously.

The more your children respect you and trust you, the safer they are under your care. The greater your influence.

Some parents want to believe that they had absolutely nothing to do with their children's drug involvement. That's bullshit.

Some parents want to take full blame for their children's problems, as though there were no other influences in the lives of their offspring. That's stupid.

But every parent plays a major role in his child's development. From day one, the child is tuned in to his parents' feelings. The parents' attitudes, beliefs, commitments, and value system become the child's heritage.

What impresses a child about his home and family absolutely affects his development.

What the child chooses to remember and what he tries to block out of his conscious mind are important factors in determining what kind of adult he will eventually become.

I'm not saying that the parent is the only influence in the child's life. His peers, his teachers, his environment play a major role in his development. A researcher recently said that by the time a child is seven or eight years old, parental influence slips from first place to maybe second or third. His peers, we are told, become number one. It doesn't have to be that way!

Too many parents relax when the kid is old enough to get to and from school by himself. They think that they can turn the job over to the school and the teacher. Well, let me tell you something, most teachers aren't going to take over any of the parents' responsibilities for them. It ain't in their job descriptions. Thank God if they teach your kid to read and write. Don't expect them to support your values or worry about your kid's morals or build his self-esteem. That's something the parent has to do, and if he relaxes the child is going to slip. You can bet on it.

When a child begins associating with his peers, without his parents around, he puts into practice a lot of what he learned in the home. It's his training ground for the adult world. What he learns from his peers is important. Which characteristics he adopts from them is very important. And what he learns about relationships and about himself is critical in his development.

The caring parent makes it a point to know what is happening to his child during this important period. The child needs his parents to lean on and for guidance and for love.

If the child doesn't get these things from his parents he'll get them from someone else, and the price he may have to pay can be incredibly high.

There is always someone in the school yard who is ready, willing, and able to be the number one influence in your child's life if you abdicate! Some kid who yours will look up to. Usually it's someone who is bigger and stronger or prettier and more popular.

If you don't set down the guideline for your kid's behavior, you can be sure that his adopted "parents" will. They'll "tell" him what's right and wrong, and he'll accept their code or suffer their rejection. The kid who is unsure of himself, who feels insecure and unsuccessful will do damned near anything to be accepted by his peers, especially his heroes. And if your child feels unaccepted or unloved at home, he'll be willing to make any sacrifice to stay in good favor with his peers.

If a seven or eight year old turns to his peers for guidance and values, it's because his parents have relaxed their influence.

My kids know that if I see them getting out of line, I'm going to intervene. I have to—I'm their father! I love them! I listen to them. I use common sense—something they don't teach in school. You may think I'm old-fashioned and tough, but they don't. My kids know what it is to be spanked. I've restricted their activities — and I've cut off their allowance. But I never ignored them or gave them the silent treatment. And I never laughed at them when they were serious, or belittled their feelings when they were angry or jealous or frustrated. Look, I'm not perfect — raising kids isn't a science — and I've made plenty of mistakes. Sometimes I'm unfair. Sometimes I jump to the wrong conclusions and sometimes I'm tired and cranky and mean. Sometimes they got so angry at me they got tongue-tied. But they know I respect them. They don't wonder about it. They know it. And they know I love them. And one of the ways I prove it to them is never to sit on my butt and hope for the best when I see them headed for serious trouble. I intervene.

Nobody can tell me that a parent has to sit on the sidelines and watch his kids become liars, cheats, sluts, and potheads because their peers have become the number one influence in their lives. That is bullshit!

The kids who are growing up today will need all of the skills, talents and motivation that they can draw on to straighten out the screwed up society that we are leaving them with.

If the majority of them are sucked in to the blurry world of drugs I don't know what will happen to this country, and to them.

From what I see, we have slopped together a lazy, inefficient, self-centered society the likes of which this nation has never seen before. If we are going to do anything about it, if we are going to build something worthwhile out of the mess we're in, we must attack the problems right where they began. In the home.

We can blame a lot of the problems that sicken our society on the government, big business, labor, inflation, and the energy shortage, but the problems begin in the home. With the family. And the family starts with a marriage.

People don't get married "till death do us part" any more. Almost every marriage is a trial marriage, and about half of them fail. Like the houses we live in, it's easier to move into a new one than it is to repair the one we have. Why are our relationships so fragile that too often divorce seems like the only solution? Part of the problem is that relationships are something we talk a lot about, but when we get down to serious thinking, we think about Me!

I'm not suggesting that every time a couple argues every child thinks the marriage is falling apart.

It's pretty tough to keep a family whole when The Parents operate as two free independent individuals, each one seeking "personal fulfillment," each one hell-bent on doing his or her own thing.

Since most people don't know what their own Thing is, they leave their kids in nursery schools or with baby sitters or with their older kids while they run from place to place in search of It.

They may not know what their thing is or where it is, but they sure as hell know that it's not at home with their family.
Where does this leave the kids?

For one it sure as hell doesn't leave them with a sense of security. It sure as hell doesn't make them feel like they are in the mainstream of the family. They are on the outside wondering what's happening.

Sometimes they are on the outside knowing damned well what's happening.

And too often something like this is happening: Mother takes off to her Little Theatre group where she's making time with the director; Daddy jumps in bed with the lady next door, but he doesn't have to worry because her husband is in Boston running in the marathon. The kids of both families are doing all right, though. They are safe at the community center getting stoned on marijuana.

I'm not telling every kid that his parents are having extramarital sex —I am telling every parent who is fooling around, though, that there's a damned good chance your kids know it and are suffering because of it. Even if they don't know, they are suffering because of it.

Kids feel like their situation is temporary. They see families falling apart all around them, and they expect it to happen to theirs, too. They may not know the statistics, but there's at least a 50-50 chance that one day their parents will call them into a family conference and give them the bad news.

I've had kids tell me that every time they hear their parents quarrel, they get knots in their stomachs, because they think, "This is it!"

I'm not suggesting that every time a couple argues every child thinks the marriage is falling apart. My parents yelled plenty. Italians are the world champions when it comes to loud emotional fighting, but it never crossed my mind that they would ever split. I knew that my family was strong. And my kids have heard Patty and me go at it at times, but they know that our marriage is solid. Kids know. They sense it.

But what do you think goes on in a kid's head and in his nervous system when he senses that his family is fragile? I can tell you this. He doesn't feel safe and he doesn't feel every important—and usually he doesn't feel loved.

I'm not going to turn this into a marriage counseling book, but I'm telling you that kids from split homes have a hell of a lot tougher times than kids with two parents who work at their marriage. I've listened to enough kids to know that more youngsters get into drugs—and can't get out—when their family life is shaky and there are serious problems with their parents' marriage.

(Left to Right) Donna, Janice, Pat, David, Patty & Jim

Kids need loving, caring parents. And no one can tell me that when they reach a certain age they quit needing them. I needed my mother until the day she died—and my father at the age of 92 was still working at being a loving, caring parent.

I get damn sick if the stupid asses who get on the tube or write books and magazine articles expounding the "alternative life styles."

We don't need marriages, some of them say. If a couple are attracted to each other all they have to do is live together. If one of them finds someone else, he or she moves out. No big hassle. And if they brought a baby into the world while they were playing house, what then? No problem, they say, the kid will survive. I think they are sick.

An "alternative lifestyles family" appeared on the Phil Donahue Show. A man and his legal wife, maybe they were 45 or 50, their grown son and the old man's two young lovers. They were a family!

"What will happen if your husband's girlfriends have babies?" the legal wife was asked.

"Oh, I'll love them like they were my own," she answered.

The young women said they have sex with men other than the head of their family.

"What happens if they have babies by men outside the family?" everyone was asked.

"That would be wonderful!" they agreed.

Who in hell are they kidding? And why in hell would people like these be given an hour of national TV airtime to brag about such madness?

Alternative lifestyles? Cult leader Jim Jones had a great idea, didn't he? He destroyed 900 lives with it.

Communes and open marriages and Reverend Moon. What in the hell are we talking about?

There is one alternative to the way too many people are living today. A way in which our children have a chance to grow up whole, and sane and capable. It's a family headed by a husband and wife who are committed to make their marriage work—who can express their love and give their children a sense of worth. Kids need to grow up in a lifestyle that includes the teaching and demonstration of morals, values, and responsible behavior. And I'm not embarrassed to tell you that God and the sharing of a religious experience is part of the Toma family lifestyle.

Kids who aren't given straightforward behavioral guidelines by their parents feel unloved. Do you believe that? You better.

Kids who are given "things" in place of loving attention feel unloved. Do you believe that?

I don't need pollsters or sociologists to tell me that I'm speaking the truth. I get hundreds of letters every day from kids who tell me it's so.

This afternoon I went over a pile of mail that came in this morning. The first letter I opened was from a 16 year old girl who was raising herself. She has parents, but they're rarely home. They take trips out-of-town every weekend. Without her. They often go for a week or two at a time and leave her alone in their large suburban house. She's very suspicious of their activities. She thinks they are "partying" (alcohol, drugs and sex). When they go, she says, they leave her a couple of hundred dollars — and a car. She doesn't have a license but she drives anyway.

She's turned the house into a party house. Every kind of drug is brought in. Pot, cocaine, hash, heroin, booze, LSD — anything goes. Not only do all the kids in the area know this is the place to "crash," but older men are beginning to show up, too.

Here's why she wrote. She heard me talk in her school, then followed me to the next two schools where I spoke, but somehow she couldn't bring herself around to talk to me. Now she wants to go straight, but she needs help. She needs her parents, she said. But how can they help her when they live the way they do, she asked. She ended by saying, "I still love my parents. Do they love me? That's the question!"

Why in the hell should a 16 year old girl have to ask a question like that? What is wrong with people who bring children into this world, then build a life of their own that excludes them? Are they sick?

The letters in today's mail came from 20 different states. Ninety-five percent from school kids. The mix is always the same. The names change and the locations, but the cry of loneliness and parental neglect is heard over and over again. I hear it in every batch of mail and at the end of every lecture I give.

Patty and I are loving parents and our own kids respect our feelings as much as we respect theirs, but there are certain things they must abide by. We make sensible rules and expect them to be followed. They don't seem like rules anymore, they are part of our way of life— and I want to tell you we follow them ourselves! Beds are made in the morning and clothes are not left lying around. We expect anyone who uses the bathroom to clean up after himself. Everyone is expected at dinner and helps clean up afterwards. We demand respect for everyone, and we earn that respect.

We have no little kids but let me tell you something. No one leaves the house without telling us where they are going . . . and when they will be home. Patty and I do the same for the kids. They always know where we are and they know when to expect us. If we are running late, we call them. If they are running late, they call us.

I want to know who my kids are running around with. My daughters are popular girls, and they never date a boy that we don't meet first. And Jimmy always brings his girls home to meet us.

Do we sound like ogres? Well, we're not. We are caring parents and we'll keep caring as long as we live. We know that children need to live in a home, not a house. They need to know that their parents love them so damned much that they will intervene in their lives any time they think it's necessary.

I have to tell you this story about my father. He was 92 when my mother died. He insisted on living in his home alone, but he never stopped being the head of the household. My brothers and sisters

Kids need to be hugged and kissed and told that they are loved.

went a little nuts when Momma died. They fought over the trinkets she left. Not that anything had any monetary value. They loved her so much that they fought like the stuff was worth a million dollars. I'm ashamed to admit it, but I got into the act, too.

One evening I got a phone call from Pop. He hadn't been feeling well and all of us were worried about him. His voice was so faint that I could barely hear him.

"David," he whispered, "I need you right away. Hurry."

I phoned my sister. She lived close to him and I thought that she could get there before me, in case he needed emergency treatment. No one answered.

A few minutes later I was pounding on his door, and I was shocked to see how how good he looked when he answered it.

"What took you so long?" His voice was as strong as Caruso's.

"Pop, what's going on?"

"Go in the kitchen, I got something on my mind."

Everybody was there — all my brothers and sisters. No one was talking.

Poppa walked in and cleared his throat. Everybody's eyes were on him.

"You make me sick, all of you." That's how he started. "I raised a family and look what you are doing to it. You! Go sit next to your brother. You. Move over next to your sister . . ." On and on he went, making us play musical chairs. But before the evening was over Poppa put his family back together. My father, at the age of 92, never forgot that he brought a family into this world and that he had responsibilities to keep it whole. He never stopped caring for us!

Kids need their parents. They want direction, they must be given guidelines. They want strong parents, strong loving parents. Nagging parents aren't the same thing. Parents who wring their hands and act like martyrs aren't the same thing, and neither are bullies. Parents who lay down rules that don't make sense, and don't respect the value and uniqueness of each kid—aren't the same thing.

Kids need to know what behavior is acceptable and

what behavior is unacceptable by their parents and they should understand the reasons why! What is unacceptable? Tantrums, lying, cheating, disrespect, meanness, smoking pot, popping pills, having premarital sex.

Kids need to be hugged and kissed and told that they are loved. They need to know that their parents think that they are special and beautiful and nice to be with. They need to know that there are no strings attached to that love. And they need to know that rules and regulations that must be obeyed are sensible and predictable, not arbitrary and changing.

What is so tough about that? Why is it so hard for parents to express their love? Why is the number one complaint that I hear from kids always the same? They feel unloved, unwanted, unnecessary. Why in the hell should any kid in the world feel like that?

Why do so many people have trouble touching their children? We all need to be touched. It's our nature. When we don't need it and don't want it, there's something wrong with us. Something got screwed up with our personality. We need the closeness that touching brings. And kids need it badly.

Studies have been made on the importance of touching and books have been written about it. I haven't read the books. I don't need to. The kids tell me everywhere how important it is to them. I hug thousands of kids and I can't tell you how many of them tell me that I'm the first adult that has hugged them in years! That is sick. What in the hell is the matter with their parents?

Boys are more deprived when it comes to touching than girls, but plenty of girls are deprived too. For some reason when a boy gets old enough to join the Little League his parents get the idea that the kid has outgrown the need for being hugged and kissed. Too many fathers think it macho to give their sons approval with a smack on the rump, NFL style—or a love tap on the arm. Saying "Gimme five," and slapping his hands is OK, but it's no substitute for an old-fashioned bear hug. A father isn't going to turn his son into a homosexual by demonstrating his love for him. No way.

Here are a couple of lines from a letter that tear me up. It's from a 13 year old boy. "My father never touches me, but every night he sits in front of the TV with our Siamese cat in his lap stroking and scratching him. I hate them both." This boy is made to feel that he is less important to his father than the cat.

His father doesn't know yet, the kid said, but he's smoking pot and thinking about suicide. When he finds out, he'll cry out in bewilderment, "Why? Why? How can this happen?" That boy needs to be touched by his father.

My 22 year old son is a cop. He's over 6 feet tall and weighs 50 pounds more than I do, but I still hug and kiss that boy. Why shouldn't I? I love him as much today as I did when he was two years old.

None of my kids will tell a shrink that they feel unloved by their father. We have plenty of disagreements, plenty of arguments and some of them get pretty noisy, but none of them will ever question my love. The Tomas are a hugging, kissing, laughing, crying, fighting family. And none of us doubts the other's love.

Kids need love and they need discipline. They have to be held accountable for their actions. The parents must not accept bad behavior. Kids resent weak parents as much as they resent unloving parents.

Irv Levey, who's helping me put this book together, was with me in a school in Indiana. I had just finished the morning session and Irv was talking with a couple of students, two girls, one 14, the other 15. He asked them if they were going to attend the private sessions. The 14 year old, Laurie, said no.

"Why not?" Irv asked.

She told Irv that she "parties" four or five times a day and that she loves it.

"Didn't anything Toma said get to you?" he asked her.

"He got to a lot of kids, but not me. You know why? Because I don't care how I die and I don't care when I die, so I'm immune."

"What happens if you're not lucky? I mean, what happens if you don't die—if you have to live? You might get married and want kids . . ."

"Not a chance. I wouldn't bring a kid into this crummy world. My mother never should have had any children. Every time I look at her I think, 'You bitch, what did you have me for?'"

"If you're smoking 4 or 5 times a day, the chances are that you're not going to get any smarter than you are right now. Do you think that you've learned enough in 14 years to get you through your 30s and 40s?" Irv asked.

"I do all right in school," the girl insisted. "I'm an honor student."

Her girlfriend jumped in, "Laurie, you used to be!"

Then Laurie admitted that her grades had dropped dramatically since she got into heavy pot smoking. She lost interest in her school work. Couldn't concentrate. She admitted that she had trouble following the lectures, and she seemed to have trouble remembering things. She wasn't worried though—she was all right, she said.

Irv took her by the hand and led her back into the school. I was just going into the sessions room when he stopped me.

"David, talk to this girl—she's in trouble."

She turned away from me like she was going to run. I spun her around by the shoulders, then took her face in my hands.

She might have been pretty but her face was so tense and hard and her eyes so empty and pink that I couldn't tell.

"Oh my God, look at you! You're still high, aren't you?"

I kissed her on the forehead and pushed the mop of hair off her face. She was wearing a bronze marijuana leaf in her left ear. I tugged at it.

"What are you wearing that trash for? What are you advertising? That you're a pothead? That you're an easy score? Take that damn thing off and throw it away. Wash your face and comb your hair and bring your parents here tonight. I want to meet them."

Suddenly this little girl burst into tears. She pressed her face against my chest and sobbed, while at least fifty students watched.

"Please, Mr. Toma," she cried, "you be my father."

That girl wanted her parents to love her enough to put her back on track. She didn't want them to use psychology on her, or to reason with her—she wanted her parents to be at least as strong as her peers!

That evening she came back with her mother and dad. What happened to them happens to millions of families.

When Laurie started to smoke pot, they didn't pick up on it. When she was afraid of being caught, she pressed for "her own space" and they gave it to her. They allowed her to drift away from them. They didn't like it, but they didn't do anything about it. They became resigned to the situation, and they, in turn, withdrew from her. She was only 12 years old when this madness started. Had they taken her into their arms and let her know how much they loved her, they might have turned things around right away. Had they delved into her activities, found out about her friends and laid down some laws, that would have been an act of love. But they were hurt, and they were afraid. They were afraid to express their love—as though it would be a signal that they were weak. And they were afraid to take a stand for fear that they would lose her completely.

Parental love and direction go hand in hand. They can't be separated!

A friend of mine told me about a conversation he heard between a 16 year old girl and her parents, when he was visiting their home.
The girl raced through the living room and headed for the door.
Father: Where are you going?
Daughter: Not sure.
Father: Who are you going with?
Daughter: You don't know them.
Mother: What are you going to do?
Daughter: Hang out.
Father: When are you coming home?
Daughter: I have a key.
Mother: Do you have enough money with you?
Terrific! I guarantee you that if that was one of my daughters, she would never have made it through the door. She might not have made it through the night! I'd never put up with that kind of nonsense and my kids know it. Maybe that's why they never tried it on me.

Those parents weren't giving their kid guidance, they were contributing to her delinquency!

Kids need love and they need discipline. They have to be part of the family. Kids resent weak parents, especially weak fathers. And if they grow up in a home without a father, it's even more difficult for them. Out of resentment they can turn against anyone's father or any father figure. They can build up a hatred for anyone who exercises what seems like parental authority to them. A cop, maybe. A school principal. The President of the United States. The Pope. Why do you think there are so many people being shot today?

I'm not telling you parents that you are totally responsible for the problems your children have. I'm not trying to put a heavy guilt trip on you. But you have to be aware of what's happening to millions of children and you must believe that your kids may be suffering in a way that you never imagined.

Maybe you feel pretty good about yourself. Maybe your life is okay —things are working out for you. Don't assume that things are working out all right for your children.

Many of us are living on a fast track. Our senses are bombarded from every direction, from morning to night. And we suffer for it. We either make decisions impulsively, or it seems we can't make any at all.

One thing that's happened to too many of us is that we've developed a need for instant gratification. We live like we're running out of time and there isn't much in this world that's worth working or waiting for.

Instant satisfaction, that's what too many of us are looking for. Instant action and instant response. Instant relief and instant pleasure. Instant love.

This has to be part of the problem. Why so many are dissatisfied with their lives. Why so many sleazy love affairs, and why so many kids are hooked on drugs.

I want you, the parent, to be totally convinced that the epidemic exists. You must know that your child is a potential victim, if he or she isn't a victim already. And knowing that, you must become actively and passionately involved in the fight to put an end to the madness.

There's nothing wrong with marriage and there's nothing wrong with the traditional family—but there is plenty wrong with too many people who marry and have children.

Kids, if you're playing around with drugs and alcohol, you are a danger, not only to yourself, but to everyone you come in contact with. And your parents, like it or not, are still responsible for you. They have to accept that responsibility.

If you are a user, I want your parents to intervene in your life. Interfere. I want them to do everything in their power to stop you, before you destroy yourself or someone else.

You are a danger. You will try to turn your straight friends into pot smokers, and too often you will be successful. You and kids you turn on are only an inch away from turning into killers.

Do you think I'm exaggerating? Let me tell you something, it happens every day. When you read it in the papers and don't know the victims maybe you just shrug it off. But sometimes it hits close to home and you know how real the danger is.

A few months ago, a couple invited Patty and me to go out with them for dinner. They wanted to drive into Manhattan, to their favorite Chinese restaurant. I had just come home after a week in Wisconsin and didn't want to budge from my house. Besides, the family was staying in, except for Jimmy, who had a date and was doubling with another couple.

So our friends asked some people who live down the street from us to go with them, and they went.

About 8:00 o'clock Jimmy and his date stopped home. He had to change his trousers. The rear was ripped wide open. He told this story.

He and his date and the other couple went to a party. Kids were drinking beer and some of them were smoking pot. Jimmy wanted to split but the other fellow was driving and didn't want to go. Jim and his date took a walk to discuss what they would do and decided that they would get Herb (the guy they came with) to drive them home so Jim could get his car. When they got back to the party Herb and his date were high. They were sharing a joint with another couple. The four of them decided to go to a street party in our neighborhood and were waiting for Jim and his date. Jim didn't want Herb to drive but he couldn't be persuaded, so my kid grabbed the car keys out of Herb's hand and dropped them in his hip pocket. Jim turned his back on Herb and headed for the door. Herb jumped him from behind, put a headlock on him with one arm and tore the pocket right out of his pants with the other hand. He got his keys back, and before Jim recovered his senses, Herb and the other three were out the door.

The next morning (Sunday) Jim got up about seven to make an early mass. He burst into our bedroom, he was pale.

"Dad, look!" He pushed the Sunday paper under my nose and turned on the lights.

My friends had been in an automobile accident. They never made it to the Chinese restaurant. A head-on collision. The couple that had invited us to go with them were both dead. Our neighbors down the street—he was dead, she was in a coma. The car that hit them was travelling at high speed on the wrong side of a divided street.

I started to cry.

"Dad, did you see who was in the other car?"

You guessed it. The kids that Jim was with last night.

Herb and his girl were both dead. The two in the backseat were hospitalized.

Four kids were orphaned. Two kids lost their father and have a mother who will never recover. She's alive, but she doesn't know it.

Innocent peoples' lives destroyed—for what? They weren't smoking marijuana or drinking booze. Why should their lives be ended or destroyed?

I don't know Herb's parents. Probably nice people. Maybe they didn't know that he smoked pot. Maybe they knew, but figured that he had to make his own decisions, be responsible for his own acts. Maybe they thought they had no right to intervene. Maybe they tried to get him to stop, but gave up.

I don't know Herb's parents but I know this: parents have to do everything in their power to keep their kids from smoking marijuana and drinking liquor. They owe it to their children, they owe it to themselves and they sure as hell owe it to the rest of us.

Lots of people honestly believe that it's everyone's right to do what he chooses, and to suffer the consequences if he makes the wrong choices. Does that sound right to you? Well, it sounds like bullshit to me.

I don't want anyone suffering the consequences for killing me! I don't want anyone suffering the consequences for maiming my wife and children. I want them stopped before they destroy me and my family.

Too many innocent people fill graveyards—too many families are crippled for life because somebody believed that he or she had the right to act irresponsibly. Let the world beware.

People who are high are not in control of their lives. People who smoke marijuana regularly, whether they are high or not, cannot be counted on to make sound judgments, have quick reactions, or have a sense of being.

Drugs do crazy things to a person.. They destroy his pride and self-esteem. They turn non-violent people into muggers and thieves, rapists and murderers. When you can't make sound judgments you can't cope. When you can't figure things out, can't work things through, you panic. Then you lose control and God knows what will happen to you and to the people near you. I have seen the calmest people turn into raging animals after a few drinks or a hit on grass. The effect is unpredictable.

All users think that they are in control. They know that they can quit before they get into any deep trouble. They can't. The mental hospitals are full of these people. The whorehouses are filled with young girls who never suspected that drugs were getting the best of them. The big city streets are loaded with empty-headed kids wandering aimlessly, searching for their next high. At one time they thought they could beat the drugs. And the prisons. Almost every violent crime committed by a teenager is drug- or alchohol-induced.

And the graveyards are filled with the young bodies of kids who thought that they were in control of their destiny.

Let me tell you something, baby, the drugs are always in control. It doesn't matter how smart you are, how tough or how stable. You are never on top of the drugs.

You can be rich and famous and have bodyguards to keep you safe, but when you are messing around with drugs you have no protection.

I knew a boy in Hollywood—barely out of his teens—who was the star of his own television series. He had everything going for him. Handsome, terrific talent, beautiful personality, rich. There wasn't anything he wanted that he couldn't have. He began playing around with pills and almost anything else that would make him "feel good." But he was careful, he was in control. He honestly thought that he could stay on top of the drugs. He was told what I tell you—you can't fill your brain and body with chemical shit and be in control. There's no such thing as being careful when you're inhaling THC, or sloshing your brain with alcohol, or torturing your nervous system with uppers and downers, or shooting up or snorting. It doesn't matter how famous you are or how powerful you are—when you play that game you are going to pay.

This boy was no exception. The pressure of fame got to him. He couldn't figure things out. Couldn't cope. When he needed all the brainpower he could muster up, his brain wouldn't respond. He destroyed his ability to solve his problems. And when his poisoned brain gave him the signal, he stuck a gun in his mouth and pulled the trigger. Why? Why would a beautiful boy like Freddie Prinze have to kill himself?

Freddie Prinze had to kill himself. The drugs were in control of his brains—and when his drug-sick mind said "die", he responded like a robot.

Paul Newman's son wasn't protected. He died of an overdose. Gregory Peck's son shot himself to death and so did Dan Dailey III. Louis Jourdan's son OD'd. The police believed it was suicide. Jim Arness' daughter took too many sleeping pills and never woke up. Liquor and drugs killed Diana Barrymore, and Art Linkletter's daughter jumped to her death during an LSD trip. You've read plenty about Carol Burnett's daughter, and the papers have been full of the drug night-mare Mackenzie Phillips and her family have been going through. And what about the greatest entertainer in the world? He had fame and fortune—he had it all—but drugs destroyed Elvis anyway.

If any of you who use drugs think you're smarter than these young people, you better think again because

you're not. If after reading this book, you light up a joint or take a pill that wasn't prescribed to you by a doctor, you're stupid!

"If Freddie Prinze couldn't beat drugs, if the King—Elvis—couldn't beat drugs, who the hell are you to think you're going to beat drugs. You're going to go down the same way!"

I see what's going on in the schools and it tears me up. I know that what I saw yesterday and today I will see again tomorrow. But I can't get used to it. I can't sluff it off.

I don't want this country to be handed over to a generation of potheads and alcoholics. So don't get angry at me for trying to get your parents involved in your life. If you're lucky, I'll reach them and some-day you'll thank me.

Nice kids—sweet children—can go crazy when they get too much THC in their brains, or hit on a joint that was laced with dust, or ingest too much alcohol.

Nice kids can turn into killers. Like the one I told you about earlier—the boy who blew his family away after one marijuana cigarette that someone stuffed with dust.

Maybe you read about the two kids—a brother and sister—who got high after an argument with their parents. Another boy got high with them, and they bribed him into shooting their parents.

These kids will never have another argument with their parents again. They're dead. And, of course, all three have been charged with murder.

They can't believe they did it. They can't believe that they actually carried out what began as an angry fantasy. Pot can make you do crazy things.

Do you think these kids would have committed such an insane crime if they hadn't been high?

Did their parents know that their children were fooling around with dope? If they did, were they worried about it?

You read about the young violinist who was murdered at the Metropolitan Opera House. She was a nice girl and the young man who is accused of brutally murdering her was a nice boy who never got in trouble before. Do you know what his lawyer said? The kid was high. He'd been smoking marijuana and drinking beer and didn't know what he was doing. Maybe he didn't know, but that poor girl knew what she was doing when he forced her onto the roof of the building, tried to rape her, bound her and threw her down a vent shaft —alive.

Drugs and violence go hand in hand. It's impossible to separate the two. Not only is the user doing violence to himself but he's moving in a world that invites violence.

Almost every ounce of marijuana that a kid touches passed through the bloody hands of the underworld. Every kid who smokes pot is rubbing shoulders with a criminal and every parent better know it.

A 15 year old boy was using more marijuana than he could afford. He spent every cent of his allowance on it, and his lunch money. He was getting desperate. He began stealing money from home. First loose change, then a dollar or two at a time from his mother's purse. Then he got up enough nerve to go into his father's wallet and stole enough to buy a half-pound of grass. His parents never suspected him of being the thief. They blamed it on the woman who came in to clean and fired her. The kid sold half the pot to his classmates fo a good profit and he was in business.

But he ran into a problem. He was infringing on the territory of another pusher. The older boy warned him to get out of the business, but he wasn't about to. One day after school, he was jumped by the pusher and his dealer. They were doing a brutal number on him when three or four boys came to his rescue. When the fight was over, one kid was dead—a knife in his throat. One kid was blind. The same knife in his eye. Our young pusher suffered a broken vertebra and a brain concussion. A murder rap is pending.

A kid may commit a crime when he's high, but he's usually straight when he starts serving time.

The prisons are filled with nice kids—boys and girls—who would have never gotten into trouble had they stayed away from drugs and alcohol. And let me tell you, my friends, everything you ever heard about our prisons is true.

They aren't just confining. They don't simply take you off the streets for a few years—interrupt your life for a while—then send you home, good as new. No way, baby. Nice kids who just happen to kill someone in a car collision when they were high aren't sent off to a boy scout camp to pay their dues to society. That ain't the way it works. You are sent to the same prisons as the hard core criminals, the four-time losers, the lifers. You share the bullpen with them. You become their cellmates. Murderers, rapists, sadists — they will become your new friends and your new enemies. I know because I spend a lot of time visiting prisons.

When you commit a crime that sends you away, you become a member of the most violent, brutal society in the world. And unless you are the strongest, the meanest, the most cunning, you are going to be victimized like you can't imagine.

Since you're young you're going to be popular in prison. No two ways about that. You're going to be loved! The veterans are going to fight over you. They may even kill to get you. You're going to become somebody's punk.

In school you might be considered a lady-killer, in prison you are going to become somebody's "lady."

There have been cases, in prison, where young guys were force-fed female hormones to make them more attractive to their lovers.

And life is no better in the women's prisons. Young girls are brutalized by the power hungry over-sexed veterans. You are bought and sold and traded like merchandise. And sometimes abused by guards and prison employees.

If you think I'm trying to scare you, you're right. If you think I'm exaggerating to make a point, you're wrong. Last week I talked to a young man who had just gotten out of prison. He was locked up for only 60 days in a State Prison. Maybe that doesn't sound like much time to you, and it's not, compared to some sentences, but you can experience hell in an hour and lots of hell in two months.

His crime? He was picked up in a drug bust. He was a small-time dealer. He did his time.

He was brought to me because he needed someone to talk to, someone whe knows what happens inside the Walls, and would believe his story. I believed it all right. There wasn't anything unusual about it. It happens all the time.

He spent most of his time in a bullpen with about 30 other prisoners. The prison was overcrowded like all of them are — and understaffed, like always.

In the 60 days, this guy, who said he had never committed a violent crime in his life, was gang raped more than two dozen times. His body was battered, his insides shredded from the attacks.

There was nothing I could do for him. Just listen to him—and cry with him. I cry a lot. I'm not ashamed to tell you that.

One more thing about this guy. He said he never committed a violent crime. That's not true. Any time you turn somebody on to drugs, you are committing violence on that person. It it's marijuana that you are promoting, the violence is on the person's brain, reproductive system and vital organs.

Nice kids and dirty drugs. The dirt has to rub off on them.

The New York Post carried a story about a pusher who was murdered in Queens. He was bound hand and foot, tortured, then slowly suffocated. That's what the paper said. They found this guy in the john. Scribbled on the mirror with nail polish was this message, "He sells drugs to kids!"

Somebody's big brother or father took revenge. It can happen when you play with something as dangerous as drugs.

. A young man was discharged from the army, a heroin addict. He went through hell but he kicked the habit. When he knew he was straight he came home, only to discover that his sister, thirteen years old, was smoking pot everyday. He tried like hell to talk her into quitting, but she was in it deep and wouldn't listen to him. He was sickened by what was happening to her. It took a while, but he found out the name of the pusher who was supplying her with the stuff—a high school student.

One day he went to the high school and talked to the principal. He said that he was the kid's cousin and that it was important that he speak to the boy. The principal sent for him. When the pusher came into the office, the girl's brother introduced himself. The pusher didn't recognize his name. The ex-soldier mentioned his sister's name. The pusher knew something weird was going on and denied knowing the girl.

"Come on, man, you know my sister. She's one of your best customers. You sell her marijuana. You're ruining her."

The pusher began sputtering, but he didn't get a chance to argue.

The ex-soldier took a gun out from under his sweater and pumped five bullets into the pusher's head.

He laid the gun down on the principal's desk and said, "Call the police. I'll wait here for them."

I don't know anything about that high school boy whose brains were splattered all over the principal's office. I don't know what kind of a son he was or if he had a little sister. I don't know if his parents were worried about his behavior or the friends he hung around with, or where he made his money. But I know this—he'd probably be alive today if he hadn't begun to deal.

And you better believe this, every kid who lights up a joint today is a potential pusher. It doesn't matter how nice you are or how gentle you are. Maybe you wouldn't hurt another person for all the money in the world, but, baby, when that poison starts building up in your brain, it's a whole new ballgame and you are a new player. You can't predict what the poison is going to do to your personality—how it's going to affect your behavior.

And when you become a pusher, my friends, you are one of the most dangerous animals on earth. You spread disease like vermin. You are directly responsible for damaging the minds and bodies of kids who probably consider you a friend.

Pushers should be avoided as though they were lepers. Ostracized, not embraced, by their peers. They should be considered no better than child molesters or muggers who break the bodies of the old and feeble for a few pennies.

Now I'm going to say something that may sound a little crazy to you. I have talked to thousands of pushers in my life. I meet them in every single school I visit. I haven't met one yet that I didn't end up caring for. I haven't met one that is evil or bad. They are screwed up! The chemicals they've been ingesting have fogged up their brains so badly they don't know what the hell they are doing.

It's okay for me to know that, but it doesn't change the fact that I don't want them around my loved ones. I don't give a damn why they are in the filthy business of peddling drugs—they better never get near my 14 year old daughter.

Most pushers didn't intend to go into the business. It just happened. Like the last one I talked to.

She stood in line three hours to talk to me, after one of my school talks. When it was her turn to come in, she stepped out of line and waited another hour until she was the last kid I would have the time to see.

For a couple of minutes it looked like she was going to leave without saying a word.

"Do you want to cry?" I asked. "It's okay. If it'll help, I'll cry with you."

I took her hand and the contact was like a signal for her to begin crying.

"You were talking about me," she whispered, "on stage. I'm a pusher."

If you saw this kid walking down the street, you'd think she was headed for a modeling job. She was beautiful. 16 years old. Dressed like she stepped out of the pages of Seventeen.

Here's what she told me. She smoked pot only once or twice before she began dating a sharp-looking college freshman. He smoked a lot and at first she tried to get him to quit. But he was older and more sophisticated and she was afraid if she kept hassling him he'd quit taking her out. Before long she was getting high every time they were together. Then between dates. One day he told her he had made a terrific buy of some pot and talked her into taking a few lids to school with her. He'd split the profits with her. She didn't want the money, but she wanted to please him. The first bag she sold, she became a pusher. She was a popular kid and got rid of the stuff in two or three days.

He pressured her into taking larger quantities and whatever he gave her, she sold.

When she built the business up to over $500 a week, he made a date with her and brought a guy with him who was about 30 years old. He was her boyfriend's dealer. The dealer liked her and within a couple of weeks the boyfriend was cut out of the arrangement. The stakes kept getting higher and the man kept pressing more and more junk on her to sell. At some point she realized that what she was doing wasn't some casual little operation. She had connected with a major drug syndicate. It wasn't just pot that they were stocking her with now —but acid, coke, speed—you name it. They got her to get some of her friends to start selling for her — and before long she was handling between $4000 and $5000 a week—bringing in bucks at the rate of a quarter of a million dollars a year!

She was scared. The size of the game frightened her — she was making too much money, she didn't know where to stash it. She worried about getting busted. This was big time and if she got caught she would surely serve time. Her dealer kept assuring her that "his people" would protect her, but that didn't ease her mind much.

Only once did she hint that she wanted out, and her dealer's reaction terrified her. She pushed the thought out of her mind.

"I want to quit now. I never thought about the kids I was selling to. I didn't know anything about drugs except they get you high. But how can I quit? They'll kill me. I know they will."

Drugs can kill you in a hundred ways.
Your parents have to know that!

Tired and hurting—between sessions.

PART 4

HOW TO KNOW IF YOUR KIDS ARE DOING DRUGS AND HOW TO HELP THEM STOP

A few of the kids who tell me about their drug experiences say their parents know about it, but don't care.

Some say their parents had been suspicious and questioned them, but were satisfied with their denial. Some say their parents know about it, but can't do anything to stop them. But most of these kids honestly believe that their parents have no idea that they are doing drugs. They think their parents are stupid.

If there was an epidemic of chicken pox in your child's school, you'd be on the lookout for symptoms. If there was a single case of spinal meningitis, you'd have your child under careful scrutiny. Well, you better believe that drugs can have as serious consequences as any disease you can think of, and you have to believe that your child has been exposed. No child is immune. If you think that your kid is too young and innocent, too immature to be playing around with drugs, think again. Marijuana is child's play. For millions of them hash pipes and stash cans are their toys. Do you know that a kid can buy a frisbee with a hash pipe built into it? Do you know that a kid can buy a toy gun with a built-in roach clip? So don't relax because your child is too young to be smoking dope. There's no such thing as too young.

Here are some of the things you have to watch out for.

The early symptoms of marijuana smoking are behavioral, not physical. The tell-tale signs aren't obvious like the drinker's "whiskey breath," or the heroin shooter's needle tracks or the coke snorter's nose burn. What you have to look for is changes in your child's behavior.

For a lot of kids pot-smoking is probably their first serious involvement that they know their parents will disapprove of. It may be the first important experience in their lives they can't share with their parents. That puts a strain on them, from the beginning. The closer and more open the relationship, the greater the strain. They begin to worry. On one hand they don't want to hurt their parents, on the other hand they don't want to give up the new thrill they discovered. They're afraid of saying the wrong things to their folks that might tip them off. It's not an easy thing for them to deal with.

How do they manage? They avoid conversations. They spend as much time as possible in their room or visiting friends. They turn down family activities.

They separate themselves as much as possible.

Some parents are so busy doing their own thing they don't notice the change. And the kid has easy going.

Some parents notice, but misread the signs.

"Hey, the kid's growing up! Needs a little room. We gotta respect this. Gotta give him some space."

They mean well. They just don't know the difference between "a little space" and a serious split.

They may even encourage this separation. Install a telephone in the kid's room. Give him his own TV set. They think they're being good parents, but they're just stepping back when the child needs his family the most to step in.

Some parents don't shrug off this situation. They enjoy their kids and want to spend time with them. They talk to them, tell them that they love them, and won't have the family living in separate rooms. They insist the child participate in family activities. It's tougher for a child in this kind of household to do drugs.

Smart parents know that their children are being exposed to drugs, almost from the time they start school. They warn their youngsters about the hazards of drugs the same way they warn them to look both ways before crossing the street. The same way they warn them not to take candy from strangers.

The kid in this kind of family knows that his parents are more educated about drugs than the kids in the school yard. They make it difficult for him to start drugs and they give him arguments to resist the pressure.

But most kids aren't encouraged to participate in the family, and few hear anything about dope from their parents.

I've talked to thousands of kids about this and most of them tell the same thing. They think their parents are happy to give them their own space—because that way the parents get the space they want. Most of the kids I talk to honestly believe their parents are happiest when they aren't around. Think about that!

Okay, so the first change in your child's behavior that sends out a warning signal to you is his obvious attempt to separate himself from the rest of you.

Once a kid becomes a regular pot smoker he usually splits from his non-pot-smoking friends—the ones that used to come around, and maybe sleep over.

If you ask about the "old friends," your son or daughter will probably tell you that they're too babyish or boring. No fun.

The new friends may be a little older than your kid. Seem more worldly. Cool. Talk more hip jargon, dress more sloppily, appear unkempt. They usually head right for your kid's room — meet behind closed doors, record player blasting.

Your child becomes even more detached from the family. Has almost no interest in what's happening around the house, shows less affection to parents.

Your pot-smoking child will probably become more critical of your lifestyle. Find you more irritating. He'll get teed off, even hostile if you start making demands on his time and energy or if he thinks you're crowding him.

He's likely to be overtly disrespectful to you, and less careful about the language he uses around the house.

If he continues smoking pot, these early symptons generally become more obvious.

Regular smokers usually lose interest in their appearance—their hair, their clothing, their personal hygiene. That isn't always the case, but more often than not, kids who wouldn't leave the house unless perfectly groomed, de-odorized and perfumed, turn unkempt, even slovenly. Sometimes unwashed.

He's less likely to bring any of his friends around. He meets them somewhere else. Phone calls become more mysterious, callers are less likely to leave their number if the kid isn't there to take the call. If he is there to take the call and you're nearby, he'll talk in grunts and give one word responses to make sure that you have no idea what the conversation is about.

The heavy pot smoker often acts less mature than the non-user of the same age. The non-user is more aware of what's happening in the world. He's more interested in world affairs, sports, and politics. He's more concerned with family affairs. He may show more interest in his studies and talks about his future, and makes plans for them.

When a kid is heavy into marijuana, pot smoking is almost the only thing on his mind. The next "hit," the next "party," where he's going to get the money for his next purchase—that's almost all he's thinking about.

It's tough for him to hold down a part-time job, and almost impossible to deal with his future. Marijuana inhibits motivation. He's apathetic and lethargic. He doesn't give a damn! Nothing much excites him or turns him on, except the next joint.

His grades have to suffer. Previously terrific students may struggle to make average grades and average students have to hang on to keep from failing. They drop the tougher courses and try to find the easiest teachers.

Extracurricular activities become a thing of the past, unless they are a front for partying. Latin and Chess Clubs are forgotten about, and so are interests like stamp and coin collecting. Nothing interests the heavy smoker except getting high.

When a kid who has loused up his high school years with drugs gets into his senior year he may begin to panic. The fact that he is being forced to make some decisions about his life can really shake him up. The realization that he isn't prepared for the next step has to creep into his brain. The knowledge that some of his peers are ready to go to college or into the working world while he isn't is a painful pill for him to swallow.

He may begin to realize that the kids who have been so important to him—his party pals—are going to disappear, go their own way. This can be shattering. If only they could see that early on! The kids who talked him into dope in the first place aren't going to be around when he has to face the adult world. The kids who pressured him into weakening his mind with chemicals aren't going to be around when he's out in the world trying to make a living. That realization is brutal when it comes through. All that he'll get out of those relationships will be the inability to function as a whole person—the inability to reach the potential that would have been attainable had he avoided the potheads and the brain sickness they peddle.

There is lots to scare him when he nears graduation. The fact that mommy and daddy may stop being his banker looms over him like a black cloud. Lots of parents are counting the days until their kid turns 18 and gets out of high school so they can boot his butt out of the house.

The kid may begin scrambling now — trying to put something together for himself before graduation. Maybe he'll try to behave around the house, show a little affection, ask for a little advice. If he can get into some college, even a two year school, and can talk his folks into picking up the tab, he'll be buying a few more years of uselessness. He can continue living off his parents and delay the day of reckoning.

At some point the kid seems to lose all motivation, all interest in the future. He can't see beyond today.

Most of them lose their ability to concentrate and comprehend. You get the feeling they aren't "receiving" the messages you're "sending." They can't deal with complex ideas—can't understand them and can't articulate them. Often they have blank looks on their faces and their speech is expressionless.

And most of them get to the point where they have trouble remembering things. Their short-term memory seems to be short-circuited. Kids report this to me every day. Every day in every school that I visit.

Pot smokers become accident prone, and turn into terrible (and dangerous) drivers.

The user has a tough time shaking off infections and often "doesn't feel good."

169

They may complain of numbness in the limbs and torso and the side of the face.

Pink eyes and sensitivity to light are common symptoms, and the users often carry a bottle of eyedrops to hide the redness.

Pot plays hell with the lungs and the respiratory system and the smoker often coughs, wheezes, and complains of chest pains.

Marijuana can throw off a girl's regular menstrual cycle.

Sometimes a pot-smoker's mouth is so dry that he sounds like his mouth is stuffed with cotton when he talks.

They may break out frequently in rashes.

Their nostrils may be red and raw and the lining of the nose irritated from snorting narcotics or sniffing a variety of volatile substances.

The heavy pot smoker may become almost completely cut off from his family. As far as he's concerned the home has become a rooming house. A place to sleep, maybe eat, and change clothes.

He'll probably become erratic. You'll see big swings in his moods. He might be silly and giggly, then suddenly, without warning, become hostile or depressed.

At times he may break your heart with his deep depression and loneliness. At other times he may seem content to be alone, and act as if he doesn't want any relationships.

And there may be times when he'll terrorize the household with his rage and vile language. I've known kids who smashed furniture, broke windows and busted holes in the walls with their fists.

He may become suspicious and fearful, to the point of paranoia. And in advanced cases he may become psychotic.

There are plenty of things that should worry a parent and make him suspicious. When a kid comes in the house and rushes past the family and straight for his room, it may be because he's been drinking and doesn't want you to get a whiff of him—or maybe he hasn't come off a drug high and doesn't want to give himself away.

Your kid goes out with her friends and you expect her home—later she phones to tell you that she's decided to spend the night at a friend's house.

Trouble.

You can worry if you live in a college town and your child likes to hang around campus.

And, of course, there's the physical evidence. Pipes, cigarette papers, incense, eye drops, roach clips, locked boxes and drawers, drug-culture magazines, pills, seeds and stems found in pockets and purses.

Drugs cost money. In the beginning a kid will get into the scene by hitting off his friends, but eventually he has to become a buyer. They'll go after bigger allowances and more lunch money. Maybe they'll need more money for "school supplies" that they never bring home. Money may start disappearing around the house. Change first, bills later. When a kid always needs money, you can worry. And when they seem to have too much money you can worry, too.

One thing for sure, the symptoms and evidence of drug use are plentiful.

I'm not suggesting that all of these signs will appear in every case. I am saying that with the information I have given you in this book, you should have a pretty good idea whether or not your child is into drugs.

No one wants to play detective and spy on his children. In fact, most will find the idea of snooping around repugnant to them—but every parent needs to know. Your child needs you to know. The worse thing you could do is ignore or refuse to face reality—if your kid is on drugs he or she needs you desperately.

I don't know how many parents find physical evidence—sure signs that their kid's doing drugs—and either ignore it or let the child explain it away.

How many mothers have found pills or grass or a coke spoon in their daughter's purse and were happy to accept some half-assed explanation like, "That doesn't belong to me, Mommy. I took them away from a girlfriend because I was worried about her. I meant to throw them away, I guess I forgot." Parents buy that kind of crap, but only because they want to.

Parents find drug magazines, like High Times or Stone Age, in their kids' rooms, and when they confront their kids with them, they say, "Oh, the teacher assigned them to the class. I have to write a report on them." They want to believe it.

Suddenly a kid's carrying around a bottle of Murine, and no questions asked. Eye drops—that's evidence!

I'll tell you something — the kids won't like this — if I ever found anything that made me think that my kid was smoking marijuana or using any other drug, I'd make a thorough search of her room. I'd turn it upside down. I'd read her diary and her mail and I'd listen in on her phone calls. Maybe she'd hate me for it, but by God, I'm her father and I'll be damned if I won't do everything I can to prevent her from destroying herself.

I've had parents tell me that when they found out that their child was smoking pot, they had a big discussion that ended up with the kid being told, "If you feel you must smoke marijuana then we'd rather you do it in the safety of your own room than somewhere out on the streets." Do they honestly think that they're protecting their child? Well, they're nuts! There is no safe place to smoke marijuana. It doesn't matter where he light it. The THC is in the joint. And what the hell is the difference where he hits on a joint that's stuffed with angel dust, in his bedroom or on the street? Are these parents going to feel better if their kid blows his mind in the safety of his own home? I know what they are thinking. They think maybe if he's getting high at home there'll be less chance of him getting busted, or less chance that he'll hang around an undesirable element. Well, let me set you straight. If you allow him to smoke at home, the chances are that he'll smoke more grass, not less. You've put your stamp of approval on it. You're telling him that there's nothing wrong with marijuana, except that it's not legal. That's the dumbest message you can give him. You're truly contributing to his destruction.

And here's something even dumber. I've met parents who wanted so badly to get close to their kids that they smoked pot with them. They wanted to prove how liberal they were, how hep, how cool. If that's what they call parental guidance, or an act of love, then they're nuts!

Kids will respond to guidelines and sensible authority. A parent can set the guidelines and be the authority, but they have to demonstrate that they truly love their children. The kids have to know that they are loved and respected. I'm not talking about parents proving their love by increasing their children's allowance or giving them a new color TV set for their room. I'm talking about sharing ideas and letting the kids know that what they think is important.

That may not seem easy if you're going to change the course your family has taken. It can be difficult if there's a stone wall built up between you and your children. But, no matter, you have to try.

And it may be easier than you imagine. Often one honest soul-searching conversation between parents and child can start things rolling. I know kids who smoked three, four, or five joints a day and quit cold after one session with their parents. And I swear to you, hundreds of thousands of kids have quit after one day with me.

What can I do for your children that you, the parents, can't do?

Parents write to me and ask, "Why did they respond to you when they wouldn't respond to me?"

I talk to them straight and I talk to them in their language. They know that I care. I tell them the truth and they recognize it. They know that they're having problems with their memory and their comprehension. They know that they've lost their ambition and excitement. They know what I'm talking about when I tell them how many kids think about suicide. They know about the numbing sensation that's experienced in their side, their limbs and their face. They simply never connected it to their pot smoking. I know about drugs, I made it my business to know and they appreciate it.

It's true that I was addicted to tranquilizers for a while, but I never smoked marijuana or dropped acid. I never tasted liquor, not even beer. And I never smoked tobacco. But they don't think that I'm a square.

I don't try to analyze them or reason with them or intellectualize the discussion. Let the shrinks and the professors play that game. Drugs are a killer, a mind blower—that's enough reason for a kid to quit. I don't try to be civilized or to tolerate. I'm never tolerant about drugs. Drugs aren't civilized—and tolerance isn't going to stop this epidemic or rid a child's brain of THC, and all the other garbage in that joint.

Above all, make sure you're communicating.

Recently at a school I was addressing, just before talking with smaller groups of 30-50 students, a research scientist handed me a thick study on marijuana. The report condemned marijuana but you needed a dictionary to read it. I told him I wanted to show him something, and I took him into the room with me.

I read the first paragraphs of the report to the kids—total silence. I asked how many of them understood it. No reaction. I threw the report down, turned to the kids and shouted—That garbage is killing you! Stop poisoning yourselves! They got the message.

Three groups of parents are reading this book. Those who are now convinced that their children are straight, those who still aren't sure, and those who know that they're into drugs.

If you are certain that your teenagers have sidestepped the drug scene, then you and your children are blessed to have one another. If at all possible your family should get involved in an anti-drug program that's designed to help other school children. Any kid you save will not endanger your life later on.

We're in trouble, baby, this country is in trouble. And you young people have the most to lose.

If your children are pre-teens and drug-free, do everything in your power to prevent them from starting drugs. The number of elementary school kids who smoke marijuana and drink liquor is growing at a frightening rate, so teach your children about the hazards of drugs from Grade One. Get to them before the kids in the playground do.

Let their teachers know that you are aware of the drug epidemic and are worried. Teachers can help and many will, if they know that the parents really care. Don't allow a teacher to diffuse your concern by minimizing the dangers of pot. You know better. There are plenty of pot-smoking teachers and he may be one. Try to get him to read this book.

Find out how the school handles its drug problem. If you're told there is no problem, somebody's sleeping. Join the PTA and make drugs a topic for discussion. You want drugs out of the school, and you want to be sure that there is never a whitewash of it. I can't tell you how many times school administrators insisted that their system was clean, but discovered when I visited them that their schools were no different than any other, when it came to drugs.

Become a room parent if you can, visit the school and get to know the staff, get involved. If you hear of pot smoking or any other drug use in the school, make an issue of it. Other parents have to know what's going on in their kids' schools. Dammit, a kid's required, by law, to attend school and he at least should be taught in a safe environment. The more concerned the parents, the safer the school will be.

If you are not certain about your children, then you have to do everything possible to find out about them. One way is to ask. You'll be surprised how many will tell the truth if they consider themselves light users or just started . . . and if they trust you. That is, if they think that you won't come down too hard on them and make them feel like dirt. You probably won't get the truth out of a regular or chronic user. If the child is young and not too deep into it, the fact that you question him may turn him off any further experimenting. But you can't count on it. If your child denies using drugs and you have no reason to suspect that he's lying then accept his answer as the truth. That doesn't mean that you can relax and forget the problem. Your kid is going to be pressured to use drugs throughout his school years, and needs you to help keep him on the right track. You know the symptoms, keep watching for them. You know enough now to stop it in the early stages.

Remember this, most children who avoid the pressure are kids who feel pretty good about themselves and their families. They are accepted and loved by their parents — and they know it. That child is usually brought up in a home where he can't get away with bad behavior, and is never rewarded for it.

When a kid is raised without well-defined guidelines, he has trouble dealing with the guidelines imposed on him outside the home. And if he doesn't feel loved and respected at home, he'll do anything he can to get his good feelings somewhere else. As often as not, it will be at a pot party.

Many of you know right now that your child is into drugs. Others will soon find it out. All that matters now, is that you do everything possible to straighten your kid out. More than ever, he needs you now.

First of all, don't panic. If you allow your emotions to take over, your whole family may come tumbling down. You must be in control of yourself, if you are going to save your child.

After the initial shock, you will experience more than one feeling that will distress you. Guilt, for one. Many of you will cry out, "Where did I go wrong? I failed my child. It's all my fault!" Few parents maliciously neglect their children. Most do the best they can, with what they know. If you punish yourself with a heavy guilt-trip, you'll be useless to your children when they need you the most.

I met a man recently who was so depressed, and felt so guilty, when he discovered that his 14 year old daughter was using drugs, that he began drinking. Now she's an addict and he's an alcoholic. That doesn't make a damned bit of sense.

You may feel hurt and betrayed. Don't let "how could you do this to me?" be your anguished cry. Don't be a martyr. You may suffer, but you'll survive. If your child isn't turned around, he or she may not.

You may want to close your eyes and pray for the best. But you have to know that problems that are left to run their course rarely get resolved. You have to get involved. Your child's future is at stake.

You may feel uncontrollable anger. Your first impulse may be to throw the child out of your life. "You made your bed, now lie in it." That attitude may close doors that can never again be opened. You'll regret it.

You'll probably experience all of these feelings. Guilt, disappointment, hurt, betrayal, outrage. They are all honest feelings—but when you deal with your children during these difficult times, it must be with strength, compassion, and love. You must not go off half-cocked.

Confront your kid as soon as possible. Every day that you wait is going to cost him. Make time for an open-ended conversation, when you don't have one eye on the clock. If necessary, keep him out of school and take off work yourself. Nothing you or he can do is more important. Both parents should be present, even if you are divorced or separated, if that's possible. And both of you must be in complete agreement on the approach you take and be totally committed to it. There is only one thing that you want to accomplish, at this point, and that's to get your child off drugs! He must know that if he doesn't turn off drugs the consequences will be enormous. I mean this, not only in terms of his mental and physical health, but in terms of what you, as the parents, will and will not do for him from this point on.

Your approach has to be straightforward. There is no need for a long introduction. No need to dance around looking for the right opening. Don't play games. Don't allow yourself to be carried away or diverted and don't lash out in all directions. Quitting drugs—that's all you will talk about.

You have your suspicions and your reasons for being suspicious. So let your kid know what you know—lay it all out in front of him. I mean that literally if you have any hard evidence. Then brace yourself.

Your child's first reaction will probably be one of indignation, even outrage.

"What right do you have to go through my drawers? (or read my diary or listen in on my phone conversations?)".

Don't let him throw you. You did what you had to do—and what you did will never scramble his brains or destroy his future. Don't get sucked into a discussion where you are justifying your actions.

He will try to put you on the defensive.

"You never trusted me. You don't love me."

You can't deal with that now. Trusting him isn't the issue. Loving him? You're proving it right now, and someday he'll know it.

Unless you caught him in the act, the odds are that he will deny using drugs. He may say something like, "Oh, I tried it once or twice but it made me sick." Don't believe it. No matter what evidence you have—a bag of marijuana, a hash pipe or a box of Quaaludes—he will probably swear that they don't belong to him. He'll tell you that he took them away from a friend to protect him, and forgot to throw them away.

Do you know how many parents buy that story? Plenty. And you may want to. You may not want to face the fact that your kid just told you a bold-faced lie. You may even be tempted to accept his story knowing that it's a lie. Maybe you'll think, "He knows I'm on to him. That will be enough to make him quit." It won't.

At this moment, your kid will say anything, promise anything, do almost anything to get you off his case. He doesn't want you to interfere with him getting high. Getting high may be the most important thing in his life right now. Is that hard for you to believe? You must believe it, if you are going to help save him.

Realize that what you must do will turn your son's or daughter's world upside down. If you are successful he will be separated from his pot-smoking, pill-popping friends. He won't "party" anymore. He will give up the feeling of being high.

He will be forced to deal with reality, and if he's been in the drug scene very long, reality will be like a stranger to him—and one that he wants to avoid.

If he's a chronic pot smoker, don't expect him to be reasonable. His ability to reason has been tampered wih. But he can be sly and deceptive and will slip through any opening that you give him.

The message that you must drive home is clear and simple and must be communicated in a way that can't be misunderstood. It's this, "We will do everything in our power to stop you from using drugs. We will do whatever we must, no matter how painful it is for you or for us. You must stop."

Your child must know that you mean exactly what you say. He must know that you're not bluffing, and you must know it too. The actions that you will have to take will be very difficult for you. Conversation, alone, won't do the job. You gotta believe that. You must be prepared to act. Some of the things that I'm going to suggest may seem almost impossible—but you're a parent and you're dealing with your child's life.

Your child must know that you are prepared to contact the parents of his friends and tell them that your son or daughter is taking drugs, and that you intend to stop it. Toward that end, you will do everything possible to separate your child from the kids he's hanging out with. If the other parents are concerned about their kids, you'll get together with them and help each other.

Your kid must know that you are prepared to speak to his teachers and the school principal. You'll tell them that he's using drugs and will ask for their help. You want to be notified anytime he misses a class or is absent from school.

He must know that you will find out who the pushers are, and that you are prepared to notify the police and the school administrator.

Until you are convinced that he is free of drugs, you won't permit him to drive a car. Take his driver's license away from him, now.

Until he is clean of drugs, you won't give him any money that can't be accounted for. If you've given him any credit cards, take them back. If he has a bank account, take the pass book. If he needs school supplies, you buy them.

You must know where he is day and night, and who he's with. You want phone numbers where he can be reached. You'll give him a curfew and you want to see him when he comes home.

You will periodically inspect his room. You must know that there are no drugs in your home.

The kid must be given responsibilities and chores in the household. His room should be clean and so should he. The point is, you have to break the pattern in his life that has been so damaging.

Ideally, a kid who is exhibiting the symptoms of a heavy pot user should be kept under close observation for about 60 days. That's how long it takes to get the THC out of his system. One of the parents should be with him continually during this period. If the kid is still young enough to be managed, you may have to try this. It's an agonizing and expensive option (expensive, if both parents work), if the child blows his mind the cost will be astronomical, but better believe that it will take more money than you can lay your hands on, unless you're one of the super-rich.

Your kid will be going through a rough period in his life. He'll feel trapped. He may be explosive, vile. Don't stop loving him. His behavior, to a great extent, is drug-induced. Never stop loving him and never stop hating the drugs!

It takes about 60 days for marijuana's THC to leave the body. If you can keep your child away from pot that long, you'll see a dramatic change in his behavior. When he's clean, he'll understand and appreciate what you have done for him. Until then, you can expect to have your hands full. He will be desperate to get a joint, and will try any kind of trickery to get his hands on one. And he'll hate you for preventing it.

It is going to be difficult, even impossible at this point, to convince your child that what you are doing is an act of love. And it's going to be just as difficult for you to feel love for him during this period.

I'll tell you something, I'd rather have my children hate me forever, and have them drug-free, than have them love me and be potheads, alcoholics or any other kind of addict.

I can't tell you how many kids attempt or contemplate suicide. I talk to them and receive mail from them every day. Drugs are ruining their young lives. They fall behind in school; they believe that they are hated by their parents and in turn hate their parents; they discover that their party-pals aren't their friends and they have no one to turn to, to feel safe with. When they are high, they don't care. But when they come down, they are angry and confused. Mostly, they are depressed, lonely and frightened. They begin to daydream of suicide and thousands of them try it every year. Plenty succeed.

It's heartbreaking to think of children being so disappointed in life that they want to die. Many of them not yet in their teens.

How are these kids to be saved? First and foremost they must get off of drugs. Most of these kids didn't get into drugs because they were unhappy or had problems. For most, their problems and unhappiness are caused by the drugs. Many of them will be able to cope with their lives once they are straight. The others may need therapy and will respond to it after the garbage is out of their brains and bodies. You must separate them from their drugs, there is no other way! If marijuana is the primary drug that they've been using, it's going to take time. Like I mentioned before, it can take as long as a couple of months, but the poison must be cleaned out of their system. You may have to become their shadow 24-hours a day to get the job done. One parent may have to take a leave of absence from his work to do it, but there may be no other way. During this period the child needs some-one to talk to, without fear of humiliation. He needs to feel loved and cared for, but more than anything he needs to be kept away from drugs.

Too many parents are willing to make compromises along the way. If their relationship with the child improves within a couple of weeks, they let their guard down. The kid asks for the car or wants to visit his old friends and the parents, afraid of breaking the happy spell, give in.

Don't do it, no matter how tempting. I can't tell you how important it is to stick to your program, until the kid is absolutely free of the drug poison.

I have been telling you that you must not give up the fight to save your children, but what can you do if the child is in his late teens, full grown and completely out of control?

I know of teenagers who are hell-bent on destroying themselves with drugs, and are influencing their younger brothers and sisters. I know teenagers who become so violent that they smash windows, dishes and furniture, and absolutely terrorize the family. I know of teenagers who physically assault their parents. What can you do if you have a child like this?

You must be prepared to take steps that may shatter that kid's world. You may have to call the police. You can not allow your property to be destroyed and you certainly should not tolerate a physical attack on any member of your family. You may have to commit him to a mental health facility. And you may have to put him out of your house. All of these options are traumatic ones, and must be considered only as a last resort.

You must be very careful if you select a mental hospital for your child. You must find a place where he will be safe from drugs. I mean any drugs. If your kid is a heavy pot smoker, you don't want him in a facility where they will give him tranquilizers or any psychotropic drugs. You must find a place that understands the damage that marijuana does to the user.

I've come down pretty hard on psychiatrists and psychologists when it comes to their treatment of patients who are chronic marijuana smokers. They have to know that people who have a brain filled with THC can't respond to counseling and psychotherapy. Doctors have to know that psychotropic drugs can turn these kids into basket cases. You have to get the garbage out of their system before you can do anything about any psychological problems that aren't caused by the pot. I'm telling you this because I've talked to too many kids suffering from pot-sickness, who went to shrinks who didn't know a damned thing about pot. These professionals took their money week after week and never dealt with the fact that they were chronic dope smokers. So the kids kept getting worse, suffered more memory loss—experienced more numbness—and on and on.

There must be more than a couple of practicing psychiatrists who know about pot and mental illness but I haven't met them and I haven't heard about them. I know of a couple and I mentioned them earlier, but I'll mention them again. I don't know Dr. Voth at Menningers in Topeka, Kansas, but I've heard of his work and agree with the pamphlets he's written. I know first-hand about the work of Dr. Albert Honig, at Delaware Valley Mental Foundation in Doylestown, Pennsylvania. So I know that a place exists where a patient is loved and nurtured and has a real chance of becoming a whole person again—without doctors and nurses who are syringe-happy, without padded rooms and solitary confinement. If there are other doctors like Honig and other places like Del-Val let me know. I'll visit them, if I can, and spread the word, because God knows we need them.

Over the years, thousands of parents and kids have encouraged me to open a camp where kids can come to get rid of their pot-sickness. Where they can develop their self-esteem and sense of worth. Where they can find out that they can get high on life and don't need drugs. This has been a dream of mine for a long time, and one that has a chance of materializing soon.

It's a terrible thing for parents when they have to turn a child out of their house. Sometimes it comes to that. You can't allow an 18 year old boy or girl to destroy the rest of the family. I've been in homes where the behavior of one young adult caused such pain and anguish for the parents and the other children that the situation was absolutely unbearable. But, for the parents, the idea of asking the 18 year old to leave was almost impossbile to deal with. But sometimes it has to be done.

Try not to order your kid out when you are furious with him, and don't close a door on him that may be impossible to open. If a kid hasn't left voluntarily when he's out of school or of age, it's probably because he's afraid to. He may realize that he hasn't anything going for him. He may get panicky at the thought of having his money supply cut off. He may try to talk you into paying for his college, even though he barely made it through high school. Don't do it. He may try to get you to pay for an apartment and give him a regular income. Don't do it. Don't do anything to help him continue living with drugs. He must know that unless he's able to live in your house under strict rules set down by you he must leave. And when he leaves he's on his own. There's an outside chance that if you set down the rules and let him think about it for a day or two, he may follow them. But the chances are, he will reject the rules, and leave.

I've known of kids who were forced to leave their homes and returned a few weeks later with an attitude that was acceptable to their parents.

It's a risk, but one you may have to take. If you let such a kid stay home, on his terms, there is no risk—you are sure to lose him.

It's a maddening decision to make, but when a kid is of age and impossible to manage, you have to force him into facing the world on his own.

Before I start talking directly to the kids again, I want to emphasize a few of the points that I made along the way.

Too often we get our values all screwed up. We confuse money and status with happiness. There isn't a thing that you can give your children that's more important than your love, your guidance, and your attention.

Every child needs parents. But not just any parents. They need loving, caring parents who have a fix on their priorities and place their kids high up on the list.

If you are part of a two parent family, the greatest gift you could ever give to your children is to make sure that their mother is home when they come home from school. I know that it costs a lot to live today, but I also know that most married mothers who work, aren't doing it to provide the necessities. They do it to provide the luxuries.

Recently I met with a family—parents, 14 year old daughter, 11 year old son. The fifth member of the family left home when she was 16 years old, pregnant. They hadn't heard from her since. The 14 year old worries the parents. She's running around with a crowd of older boys and girls, and they're afraid that she'll end up like her sister.

"Why do you work?" I asked the mother. She's a legal secretary.

"We need the money. We can't get along on one salary," she said.

As it turned out, the money she earned wasn't used to help feed, clothe, house, or educate the children. Her salary was paying for a recreational vehicle, an 18 foot cabin cruiser, his and hers trail bikes . . .you get the idea. Those luxuries are no trade-off for the children who need their mother at home. They need her when they take off for school in the morning and they need her when they come home in the afternoon.

Getting your priorities in order . . . it's the easiest way to save your children.

In my family dinner time is really important. That's when we're all together. We don't eat on the run. That meal is an event, even if we're having leftovers from the night before. What makes it important is our conversation. Sometimes it keeps us at the table an hour or more after we've finished eating. We exchange stories and experiences and rap about anything that's on anyone's mind.

Patty and I often go to bed earlier than the kids do, but sometimes we can't keep the kids out of our room. Many evenings they are all over our bed, yakking and kidding around. Sometimes they invite their friends in and it's like a nuthouse. I yell at them, "For crissakes get out of here, I'm old and need my sleep!" But they know what I'm thinking. "I love you and I'm proud that you want to be with your mother and me."

You will have to make sacrifices. That's part of parenting. You will have to cut back on some of the activities that separate you from your children. Sitters are okay occasionally, but they can't raise your children. And your kids can't raise themselves.

Demonstrate your values. Don't underestimate your children's ability to recognize the truth. They know when you're dishonest. They know when you're cheating on your spouse. They know when you're hooked on drugs or alcohol.

One way to demonstrate to your children just how serious you are about putting your family together is to give up your chemical crutches. Make it a family project. They have to quit drugs, you quit tobacco and alcohol.

Everyday I'm asked how do you help someone who's on drugs? The four basics are:

One—You've got to be straight yourself—you can't be playing the game that you're telling other people to quit.

Two — You got to know what you're talking about. They'll never respect you if you talk about drugs without real understanding.

Three—You have to care and show them that you love them and are genuinely concerned for their welfare.

Four—You must have the patience of a saint. Never, never give up. It took me 28 years to get one of my nephews straight but he's doing well today.

Get together with other parents who are experiencing similar problems with their children. There are lots of concerned people who are banding together to protect their kids. Organizations are forming in every part of the country where I've spoken. For example, in Salem, N.H., a Toma group provides trained people to combat drug and alcohol abuse. In Coral Gables, Florida, "Youth Crime Watch," composed of students from 40 Miami high schools, meets to fight drug abuse problems. In Reno, Nevada, "Operation Toma," consisting of over 135 citizens, offers their services to various drug abuse organizations. In Cedar Rapids, Iowa, P.R.I.D.E. (Parent Resource and Information in Drug Education) provides literature, a volunteer hot line and help in educating parents on drug abuse. If you want to locate one of these groups in your area or start one, write to me for information.

You can help save your child's future. The alternative can be brutal. They need your love and commitment. Your love and commitment—not your doting, not your anger, not your fear, not your education, not your money, not your achievements, not your faith, not your pain.

PART 5

Kids—I'm counting on you to quit drugs NOW!

Kids, I'm not writing this book because I'm worried about your parents' future. And I'm not concerned about mine either. I'm a survivor and I'm doing all right.

I'm writing this book because I love you, and because I love this country.

What I see happening to you terrifies me. Organized crime has zeroed in on you. They have made you their number one target. You are their future and so far they've had everything going their way. They're feeding you poisoned candy and you are being hooked on it.

They don't give a damn about you.

They don't care if they cripple your mind or your body.

187

They don't care if they kill you. They'll replace you with your little brother and sister. They will get them just like they got you.

I am afraid for you and I'm afraid for this country. The criminals and their drugs are turning us into a second or third class nation. They're robbing us of our talent, our intelligence, our ability to perform.

It's no secret that this nation has enemies, and those who hate us are jumping with joy to see what drugs are doing to you.

It doesn't matter how much of our tax money is poured into the defense of our country. It won't mean a damn if we have the most sophisticated weapons money can buy, unless we have the human capability to operate them. Do you know who is protecting this country today? Thousands of high school graduates and drop-outs who carried their habit into the service with them. You better believe this — the majority of the young men and women in the armed services today get high regularly. What in the hell good are they going to be in case of an emergency? We're kidding ourselves if we think the billions of dollars we're spending for defense is going to protect us.

We're in trouble, baby, this country is in trouble. And you young people have the most to lose.

Our foreign business competitors have to be tickled pink with the job that the drug peddlers are doing to us. How in the hell can potheads and addicts produce quality merchandise to compete in the world market? We used to be the leaders in the world when it came to quality. Something tagged "Made in the USA" was respected. Today we're the number one customers for foreign producers. Hell, we don't want to buy the junk that's being produced in this country. One of these days the big corporations will wake up and get rid of every pothead, coke snorter, and alcoholic that's on their payrolls.

We are sick and we are getting sicker.

I don't want potheads taking care of me when I'm hospitalized. I don't want them flying our airplanes. I don't want them driving our buses and subway trains. And one of these days we're going to get them out of government, and out of the legal and medical professions.

We are so sick and it scares me.

No one can put an end to the epidemic of madness that is strangling us — but you. You are our only hope. If enough of you make up your mind that you're not going to trade in your life for a chemical high, we'll have a chance. If enough of you decide that you're not going to allow the producers, distributors and pushers of drugs to turn you into mental and emotional weaklings, we will have a chance.

Band together now and force the pushers out of your schools, and out of your lives. These people are spreading a disease that in many cases is incurable and in every case is damaging. You've got to believe that. Your life depends on it.

Make up your mind, today, that regardless of what anyone else does, you are going to save yourself. No one can do the job for you. You have to do it yourself.

Give yourself a chance to live and to grow. You are worth the effort.

"Now it's up to you, friend. What's it going to be—that garbage or your life? I care what you do! I want you to start respecting and loving yourself today — to start living."

Quit drugs right now. Let your last high be the very last. Know, right now, that you will never again put that garbage in your body.

Never again put poison in your brain. From now on consider anyone who tries to tout you on to drugs as your enemy. If you want to give them the benefit of the doubt, then consider them stupid asses who aren't worth listening to.

Don't waste your time and energy debating the pros and cons of marijuana. There is nothing anyone can say in favor of grass that is valid. In all my years of fighting drugs, I've refused to debate the pro-pot people. You know why? Because they are assholes, they are killers. Every now and then I'm invited to appear on a talk show to argue with some representative of one of the pro-marijuana organizations. The producers think that a debate will increase their ratings. I tell them to shove it. To me they are as bad as thieves and murderers. I wouldn't sit on a panel with a sex offender and argue the pros and cons of rape. There are no pros. So don't argue with anyone who uses drugs. If they are willing to listen to you—fine. But don't listen to them.

There is only one way to quit and that's cold turkey. There is no such thing as tapering off. You can't have one last hit "for the road." You just quit.

I have thousands of letters from kids who quit, and everyone did it cold turkey. Plenty of them were heavy users. Some said they had stayed high around the clock — smoked six to eight joints a day, popped speed, snorted coke and quit cold.

If you can say the words, "I quit. I will never do drugs again," you've got it made.

Quitting requires action. Here are some of the things that you have to do.

Get rid of all the junk that you have stashed away. Don't give it away, and for God's sake don't sell it—flush that garbage down the toilet!

Every day that I talk in a school, kids empty their pockets and purses of the shit that they've been using and send it down the drain. You do the same thing. You'll get high watching that poison disappear, knowing that it will never damage you or anyone else.

Now get rid of all your drug paraphernalia. Take a hammer and smash your pipes and bongs, spoons and clips. Bust up your stash boxes and if you have any drug-jewelry throw it in the trash along with those drug-magazines!

Get rid of all that shit. You don't need it. You're no junkie.

Now get on the phone. Start calling your closest friends. Tell them what you just did. Ask them to join you. Tell them that you'll never get high again and that you have to break away from those who do.

Coax them into quitting. Loan them your copy of this book and insist that they read it. The more friends that you can convince to band together with you, the more fun quitting will be. But more importantly, you will be proving that you are a true friend.

But no matter what, you must stick to your guns. You must not hang around the kids who continue to play with drugs, and your friends must know it.

If your parents know that you were doing drugs, or suspect it, call a family conference. Tell them that you quit. Don't be ashamed. It will be an act of love on your part that they will never forget. I've come down pretty hard on a lot of parents who lost their kids to drugs. Most of them would give up their lives to save their children. I've talked to many of them and I can tell you they suffer incredible pain—and, too often, blame themselves for their children's troubles. If drugs got between you and your parents, make a special point to let them know that you love them. They need all the support they can get.

Talk to your teachers and principal. If there isn't any anti-drug program in your school that includes students, parents, and faculty, urge them to start one.

More than anything else, stay away from the drug users. Let the pushers know that you want no part of them. Keep away from these kids as if they were lepers. And under no circumstances should you attend a pot party. THC is not only in the smoke that is inhaled, it's also in the smoke that is exhaled. And that THC will sure as hell get into your bloodstream.

Do something with yourself! Walk, run, exercise. Keep busy. Get into music; sports that you might desire; drink a lot of fluids—water, fruit juices—no alcohol. Much of the garbage and poisons will be removed from your body by the exercise and fluids.

Have a real party! Celebrate with the kids who are now straight. Prove to yourself that you can get high as a kite without booze or beer or drugs. For a lot less than the cost of that kind of garbage, you can have a hell of a party.

You'll find out what a terrific person you can be, when there is nothing in your brain to fog it up. You'll have more energy, be more conversant, and a hell of a lot more attractive.

Be patient with yourself, especially if you have been heavy into pot. It will take time for all the THC to work its way out of your body—maybe a couple of months. But it won't take long before you begin seeing improvements in the way you feel, your attitude and your behavior.

If you are now experiencing some episodes of "drifting," flashback or memory loss, don't panic. Just stay away from drugs and the conditions are certain to improve. If you're lucky, the symptoms will disappear completely.

In time your ability to concentrate, read, and comprehend will improve. And so will your schoolwork.

Your relationship with your parents will certainly improve—even if they are absolutely wacky. Let me put it this way—there are plenty of screwed-up parents in this world. The more together you are, the easier it will be for you to cope with them. Don't ever do anything to harm yourself, to spite them. Try to be a positive force in your family. Most parents love their kids—some never learned how to express their love. If you have parents like this, try to reach them—tell them what you think is wrong with your relationship. Tell them of your needs. If they don't show you affection — and I mean hugs and kisses — ask them why not? You may be able to reach them or teach them.

Learn to love yourself. Give yourself reasons to love yourself. The more you reach out and try to help someone, the better you will feel about yourself. You need good feelings. You need good thoughts. And when you hate, hate something that deserves that kind of attention. Hate drugs and pushers, hate lying and cheating and crime.

Most of us have a tough time loving ourselves — but when we begin to realize just how valuable we are, we begin to find out what a real high is. And I'll tell you something, the more you learn to love yourself, the more respect you give to yourself, the easier it will be for you to love and respect others.

It's an incredible thing to be able to look in a mirror and say, "Hey, you're really all right. I love you," and you'll know what those words mean when you say them to somebody else.

As soon as you've made the commitment to yourself to quit drugs forever, look in a mirror and say those words, "You're really all right. I love you." You'll begin to feel what I'm talking about.

I don't know what you kids are going to do when you close this book. Plenty of you will quit drugs, but some of you won't give a damn about anything I've said in this book. I can't force you to quit.

I'll pray for you though. I'll pray that if I failed to reach you, someone else will get to you before you blow your mind forever. I'll pray that something will happen to make you stop before you lose your memory, before your brain is incapable of taking in new information, before you lose the ability to manage your life. I'll pray that something will stop you before you are incapable of having a normal child.

If you think that you can continue using drugs and one day walk away from them undamaged, you are a stupid ass. You can't beat the drugs. Don't let anyone tell you differently. The drugs beat you!

You will be a loser, and when you've lost, not one of your "party" friends will be around to give you a hand. They will disappear from your life as though you never existed. They aren't going to give you the time of day when you're down in the gutter. People who are hooked on drugs have no friends. Playmates and co-conspirators, but no friends.

You're no tougher or smarter than Freddie Prinze or Elvis Presley or the thousands of others who destroyed their minds and bodies with drugs. What in the hell will it take to awaken you? Are you too sick to understand the message in this book? Has the THC got your brain so clogged up that it can't accept this information? How close are you to your saturation point? How soon before you become a street junkie, or a prison inmate, or a patient in a mental institution, or a name in an obituary column?

I want you to live.

It doesn't matter, at this point, why you started using drugs. What matters now, is that you stop. You didn't know what you were doing to yourself, but now you know. You can never again be innocent of the facts. If you continue now, you have no respect for life.

Girls, quit drugs today. Respect your body and your mind. Be proud of your womanhood. You'll be sorry if you don't. I've never met a pot-smoking female who was a lady. I've met plenty who were whores and sluts and shoplifters and petty thieves. I've met plenty who talked as filthy as any hardcore criminal, but I haven't met one, who a child would be proud to have as a mother.

Quit today. If you are into drugs, you're probably sleeping around too. If you're not, it's only a matter of time. Drugs drag your morals down to the gutter. They screw up your values so badly that you don't know right from wrong. You must respect yourself if you are going to make anything of your life. And you can't respect yourself if you are a pig. You're not going to end up with any of the potheads that you're giving yourself to. In five years you won't remember their names and they sure as hell won't remember yours. Boys talk. They brag about their conquests. A girl trusts one, and when he's finished spreading the word about her, she sounds like a sex-crazed nymphomaniac. You don't need that. The real world isn't the way <u>Playboy</u>, <u>Penthouse</u> and The <u>Hustler</u> portray it. They want you to believe it, but they are sick. That isn't the way the world is for Patty, Donna and Janice Toma. And it needn't be your world either.

Do you want to experience a real high? An incredible ego-trip? Tell the next guy who wants you to get high with him to shove it! Then keep saying it everytime one of those bums get near you. You'll start feeling clean again. You'll feel like a heavy burden has been lifted off your back. You'll see a new, bright, beautiful face shining back at you when you look in the mirror.

If you have a steady boyfriend, try to help him. Tell him that you are done with drugs, and that you will not go with anyone who gets high. Tell him that you will not see him, until he is clean. You'll find out soon enough how important you are to him. If he chooses drugs over you, you know where you stand — and be glad that you found out. No respectable girl can afford to run around with a guy who doesn't respect her or himself. And no one who turns his body into a garbage can for drugs is respectable. Demand respect from the boys you go with!

Boys, you may not believe this, but drugs and manhood are not compatible, Guys who need chemicals to make them feel manly are only imitating men. I've seen plenty of potheads who are bullies, muggers, and rapists, but none who was a man. Put them up against a real man and they turn into snivelling cry babies. I've been up against thousands of them in my life, as a cop and in my work today. They may stick a knife in your back, beat the hell out of an old man, or rough up a 90 pound girl, but I've never seen one who would take on a real man, face to face. And let me tell you something else, if you think that drugs make you sexy, you're kidding yourself. Keep getting high and in time you won't know the difference between a woman and a watermelon. Drugs can't make you strong or brave or virile. They make you weak and cowardly, stupid, and impotent.

The bravest kids in your school are the ones who thumb their noses at drugs. That takes guts, and it will pay off for them. When those of you who continue getting high are thirty years old, and still scrounging for your next hit, they will have homes and families and careers.

Join me, today, in the fight to bring an end to this insane drug epidemic. Decide, right now, that you will quit drugs. Make a commitment that you will never again be a patsy for the criminals who are making billions of dollars poisoning your generation of kids. Make up your mind, now, that you will walk away from the drug society and never look back.

I am asking you now to join me.

Well, that's it. I mean I've finished this book. With all my heart I hope that I've helped to turn you off drugs. Now I want you to do something for me. Will you write me? Let me know how you're making out. I promise that I'll read your letter. Share your successes with me, or maybe you just need an ear.

Write to: David Toma, P.O. Box 854, Clark, N.J. 07066.

There's a good chance that we'll meet. I talk in schools almost every day of the school year and I cover almost every part of the United States. So if I'm in your town, or near it, make it your business to say hello.

Before you close this book, I want to give you a gift. It is a gift that my mother gave to me when I was a little boy. I could have it, she said, only so long as I was willing to share it with others. I cherish that gift, and because I had it, I joined the police department and fought to make the streets a little safer—because I had it, I fought to make the police department a little more compassionate — and I fought Hollywood and the media—because of her gift, I spend 16 hours a day in schools from coast to coast—and I wrote this book.

What my mother gave me and said that I must share, is her love. And so I share it with you. And I give you my love, and ask that you share it with others. I love you. I'm not ashamed to tell you. I love you all! And God bless you.

POSTSCRIPT

On July 24, 1981, as this book was being written, the American Medical Association (AMA) made the following statements in a press release:

"There is now no doubt at all that marijuana is a dangerous drug, with great potential for serious harm to young American users . . . marijuana is by no means the harmless amusement that many believe it to be . . . .

Target organ for marijuana is the brain. Structural changes occur in the brain with marijuana use, as well as changes in the patterns of brain waves. Acute marijuana intoxication impairs learning, memory, thinking, comprehension and general intellectual performance. Even at moderate levels of social use, driving skills are impaired. . . .

Chronic use of marijuana may be associated with disruption of the menstrual cycle and at least temporary infertility. Miscarriage is more common among users. Among lab animals, sperm abnormalities have been noted, along with damage to the male reproductive organs.

Many physicians experienced in treating drug abusers believe that regular marijuana use may seriously interfere with psychological functioning, personality development, and emotional growth and learning, especially in childhood and adolescence. The psychological damage may be permanent. Large doses of THC can induce hallucinations, delusions and paranoid feelings. Thinking becomes confused and disoriented. The initial euphoria may give way to anxiety reaching panic proportions.

Even moderate use is associated with school drop-out, psychoses, panic states and adolescent behavior disorders. . . .

The American Medical Association is clearly on record as opposing legalization of marijuana for recreational use.

Legislators should keep in mind the primary need to give young people a clear message that marijuana use may be hazardous and is not sanctioned or endorsed by society."

My first reaction was, 'What the hell took them so long? I've been saying that for 20 years!'

But at least now the prestige and power of the medical profession are lined up on the right side of this battle—where they belong. It will be more difficult for quacks to lull people into a sense of complacency over marijuana, that is as soon as they learn about what the AMA said. I heard about it on the radio news—but The New York Times, The New York Daily News, The Chicago Tribune, the Newark papers and the L.A. Times did not carry the story! What has to be one of the biggest developments of the decade—and they didn't cover it. In fact, I don't know of any newspaper that carried it! Why?

Friends, if the media won't cover the message of how dangerous marijuana is, then in self-protection we have to broadcast it ourselves—to our families, friends, associates, and all those who need to hear it. I'm counting on you.

What students say about TOMA:

All of the following quotes are excerpts from the hundreds of thousands of letters people have sent to David Toma.

"When I first heard you were coming I laughed. I wasn't going to let some know-it-all cop change my life. When you walked onto the stage I laughed and said 'Who in the hell does he think he is?' When I walked out of the gym, I wasn't laughing. I was crying. I went right to the bathroom. My drugs and rolling papers went down the toilet. Why did I respond to you when no one else could reach me? I think I know. You know what you're talking about, first hand. I know you believe every word you say, and I believe you. And most of all, I honestly believe you when you say that you love us kids. And I hope you know that we love you too."

"How do you get your parent's attention? No matter what problems I have, they say 'Work it out.' "

"There are six kids in my family. Four are doing drugs. I can't make my brothers and sisters quit but I have made up my mind that I'm not going to destroy myself. I love you for giving me back to me."

"My parents never would even dream that I smoked pot. So after the parents night I got them both together and spilled everything. They said that they were glad that Toma came and that they respected me for telling them. I feel a whole lot better now that it's all behind me."

"I'm so proud of myself! Tonight these 2 guys asked me to smoke some pot with them and I turned them down and told them I didn't do that crap anymore. You wouldn't believe how great I felt after that. My mom and I always fought about drugs but she couldn't turn me off of them. She can't understand why I quit for you! I tried to explain that she always threatened me and tried to make me feel like dirt, but you made me feel really good about myself."

"I am a housewife and mother of two elementary school children. I was making arrangements to have an outsider look after my children so I could resume my career. After hearing you speak I am convinced that I'm doing 'my thing' right at home. The business world can get anyone. My family can only get me."

"When I was sitting in the bleachers listening to you I decided to give it all up. Booze, pot, beer, cigarettes, everything. And I am really happy. I told my boyfriend, who is what you call a pot freak not to show up at my house again and I turn down every party I'm invited to. I'd only been into drugs for a little over a year and I feel terrific now that I quit! I've taken up jogging, like you said, and in a way I kind of get high off running. When I'm out of school and reach my peak, I'm going to try to help people like you do."

"My right side goes numb once in a while but I never connected it with marijuana. My mother has been telling me for years that I may be ruining my chances for having children but I never listened to her. I guess it takes someone like you to make teenagers listen."

"I smoked pot, and took speed, barbs, but I quit because what you were saying. Most of my friends have quit too. The teachers here are putting you down but I think and the other kids think that you are wonderful because you got us to quit."

"You have saved many lives including mine. I OD'd, I supplied Cocaine, I have now stopped dealing and started helping. You made me realize that I am loved. I have never felt the way I did until I heard you. Many tears were shed. I got the shit kicked out of me for going straight, but I'm hanging in there and I damn well plan to stay that way. God must have sent you because you are a miracle worker."

"I thought maybe by taking drugs and smoking pot would get me accepted by the 'head' group. It did, and now I don't like it. I used to be an A student now all I think about is getting high. When I have a bad day in school I take a hit of mescaline, but when I come down I'm more depressed than ever. I'm only 16 and I know that I'll be okay if I quit right now and that's what I'm going to do."

"You made me think seriously about what I want out of life and to realize that I should be more considerate and helpful to others. Our school now has a 'Toma Club' where we can talk freely about out problems with people who care."

If you would like to order additional copies of this book, please send a check or money order as follows:

1 copy—$4.00 plus $1.00 for postage
                & handling
2 copies—$8.00 plus $1.00
3 copies—$12.00 plus $1.00
4-6 copies—$4.00 each, plus $1.25 for
                     postage & handling
7 or more copies, $4.00 each, postage
& handling free.

For orders of 100 copies or more, write for
prices on quantity discounts.

New York residents please add applicable
sales tax.

Mail To:
JAN Publishing
c/o McCafferey Enterprises
15 Oakland Ave.
Harrison, New York 10528

Name _____

Address _____

City _____ State _____ Zip _____

If you would like to order additional copies of this book, please send a check or money order as follows:

1 copy—$4.00 plus $1.00 for postage
        & handling
2 copies—$8.00 plus $1.00
3 copies—$12.00 plus $1.00
4-6 copies—$4.00 each, plus $1.25 for
        postage & handling
7 or more copies, $4.00 each, postage
& handling free.

For orders of 100 copies or more, write for prices on quantity discounts.

New York residents please add applicable sales tax.

Mail To:
JAN Publishing
c/o McCafferey Enterprises
15 Oakland Ave.
Harrison, New York 10528

Name _____

Address _____

City _____ State _____ Zip _____